The Racehorse in
Twentieth Century Art

THE
RACEHORSE
— IN —
TWENTIETH CENTURY ART

CLAUDE BERRY

Foreword by The Earl of Halifax

· THE ·
SPORTSMAN'S
PRESS
LONDON

Published by
The Sportsman's Press 1989

© Claude Berry 1989

British Library Cataloguing in Publication Data
Berry, Claude
The racehorse in twentieth century art.
1. Visual arts. Special subjects. Racehorses
I. Title
704.9′432
ISBN 0-948253-34-7

Photoset and printed in Great Britain by
BAS Printers Limited, Over Wallop, Hampshire

Contents

Acknowledgements

The appeal of a book of this type lies as much in the illustrations as in the text and I would therefore like to thank the owners of the pictures shown here for their permission to reproduce them. I hope I will be forgiven if I have been unable to trace the owner of every picture. I am grateful to all those artists who have lent me photographs of their work and to the following who have been most helpful in providing illustrations: Arthur Ackermann and Sons Ltd., the Court Gallery, the Anthony d'Offay Gallery, the Fine Art Society, Frost and Reed, the Richard Green Gallery, the Heale Gallery, the Jockey Club, the William Marler Gallery, the Sir Alfred Munnings Art Museum, W. H. Patterson, Marie Pritchard-Jones, the Richmond Gallery, Alastair Simpson, the Sladmore Gallery, the Oliver Swann Galleries and the Tryon Gallery. Among others who have kindly helped me I would like to single out Mrs John Skeaping, Mrs Stella Walker, and Gillem Sandys-Lumsdaine.

I am greatly indebted to Miss Marjorie Edwards who very kindly vetted the chapter on her brother and to Mrs Peter Biegel who did the same for the chapter on her husband. I would also like to thank Dolly Bennett who handled all the correspondence with unfailing initiative and cheerfulness and, finally, my wife, Meg, who typed the manuscript at unbelievable speed and made many very helpful suggestions.

C. de P. B.
Tiverton, Devon.

List of Illustrations

ILLUSTRATIONS IN THE TEXT

Foreword by
The Earl of Halifax, JP, DL
Chairman of the British Sporting Art Trust

As Sir Alfred Munnings once remarked with sadness to Lionel Edwards 'Those who know about horses know nothing about art, and those who know about art know nothing about horses.'

Claude Berry knows something of both fields. On leaving school he worked in a racing stable and subsequently rode for ten years with success as an amateur under National Hunt rules and in point-to-points. He also trained under permit and, when his race-riding days were brought to a conclusion following a bad fall at Sedgefield, started a small stud in Scotland. He bred several flat and jump winners and was one of the first small breeders' representatives on the council of the Thoroughbred Breeders' Association. He has also acted as a steward at Hamilton, Carlisle and Kelso.

He has been a director of the Tryon Gallery since 1980, is on the executive committee of the British Sporting Art Trust and is the art correspondent of *The European Racehorse*. He also writes for *The Field* and contributed the chapter on twentieth century pictures to *Collecting Sporting Art* which was published in 1988.

It is therefore not surprising that he has assembled a splendid collection of racing paintings and sculpture to illustrate perhaps the first overview of twentieth century racing art to be published in such a substantial form. Followers of racing and collectors will surely relish the many fine examples of the work of Munnings, Edwards, Lyne, Skeaping, Crawford and Blacker among many other artists and sculptors whose work is reproduced here.

Halifax

Charles Simpson, *Golden Miller at Aintree.*

George Wright, *Two Furlongs Out.*

Introduction

The greatest problem in writing a book of this type is to decide which artists to include and which to omit. As a general rule I have included only those whose racing pictures form a significant part of their total output. This means leaving out the recognised hunting painters George Wright (1860–1942), George Derville Rowlandson (b.1861) and Frank Algernon Stewart (1877–1945), whose racing pictures were few and far between. Omitted for the same reason are the highly talented Lucy Kemp-Welch (1869–1958), Charles Simpson (1885–1971) and Edward Seago (1910–1974) who painted, in addition to his marvellous landscapes, a small number of superb racing oils. I have, however, included a few examples of the work of these artists (*see Plate 1*).

I have also tried to avoid the temptation to enthuse about certain contemporary artists whose work is often too lavishly praised by their agents and friends but which will be largely forgotten in years to come.

The main danger is in attempting to pronounce judgement on a century which still has more than ten years to run. It is perhaps as foolhardy as attempting to forecast the result of a race when the leaders are still a furlong from home. Tucked away in the pack of younger artists today there may well be one or two talented outsiders who will come with a late run during the next decade to establish their reputations. We shall see . . . .

Joseph Crawhall, *The Racecourse*.

ONE

The Early Years

In 1900 six artists, all in their thirties, had already started to establish reputations which were to increase as the century progressed. They were a disparate group, linked by little more than the decade of their birth and the fact that much of their artistic inspiration came from the horse. The six can conveniently be divided into three pairs: Joseph Crawhall and Robert Bevan were the most talented and original of the sextet; Lynwood Palmer and Alfred Grenfell Haigh were painters engaged mainly on commissioned portraits of racehorses and hunters; George Denholm Armour and Cecil Aldin were sportsmen-artists who derived a large part of their incomes from illustrative work.

Joseph Crawhall (1861–1913) is one of the most brilliant horse painters of the twentieth century, and one of the most interesting. A member of an affluent Northumbrian family – his grandfather owned the largest rope works in the North of England and was Lord Mayor of Newcastle – he was of independent means and was thus able to draw and paint without the constraints of having to please a patron or sell his work in order to survive.

In 1882, at the age of twenty-one, he went to Paris to study under Aimé Morot, a painter of animals, portraits and battle scenes. Although he only stayed with Aimé Morot for two months, his brief contact with France and the Impressionist movement was to leave a lasting mark on him in that he threw off the shackles of late Victorian England and worked with a rarely-matched and very imaginative use of colour and form. He eschewed the use of oil paints and worked mainly in watercolours or gouache, often on brown holland. He had little use for models, his work being produced from a brilliant memory and superb powers of observation.

As a young man Crawhall went to Tangier for ten years. Together with other expatriates, he hunted with the Tangier Hounds, a mixed pack whose quarry consisted of fox and pig and whose master was an Old Etonian Spanish nobleman, the Duke

Robert Bevan, *Horse Dealers.*

George Derville Rowlandson, *1921 Grand National.*

Edward Seago, *Point-to-Point Meeting.*

PLATE 1

Joseph Crawhall, *In the Paddock.*

Robert Bevan, *Quiet with all Road Nuisances.*

PLATE 2

of Frias. Crawhall became first whip to the pack and for a time G. D. Armour was second whip. The great portrait painter Sir John Lavery was another who hunted with the Tangier Hounds at this time. A fine horseman, Crawhall won the Tangier Hunt Cup four times in succession.

Crawhall took up residence in Yorkshire at the beginning of the century. Here he bred horses and hunted with three packs, the York and Ainsty, the Sinnington and the Middleton, often riding his stallion, Beck. He was a solitary and introverted man, nicknamed, not unkindly, 'The Great Silence' by Lavery. His method of working was unpredictable: he would go for long periods without producing anything and would then work feverishly for several days on end. A severe critic of his own work, he destroyed a high proportion of his drawings. As a result, his surviving output is not large and his pictures seldom come onto the market; his superb racing pictures formed only a small part of his work and they are nowadays almost unobtainable. Much of his best work is in the Burrell Collection in Glasgow.

If the overworked word genius could be used to describe two twentieth-century sporting artists, my two candidates for this accolade would be Crawhall and Munnings. Crawhall can convey with a few deft brush strokes more depth, feeling and understanding of his subject than most artists achieve after years of painstaking labour. This brilliant and eccentric man, who during his lifetime held only two exhibitions, died in 1913 following an operation for emphysema.

Although his racing pictures were even fewer than Crawhall's, Robert Bevan (1865–1925) deserves consideration as a perceptive and unconventional horse painter. He, Crawhall and Munnings were the three equestrian artists who allowed themselves to be influenced by the Impressionist and Post-Impressionist movements and who first broke free from the conventional approach to sporting painting which was the rule in Britain before their arrival on the scene.

Born in Sussex, Bevan studied at Westminster School of Art and in Paris at Julian's. From 1892 to 1893 he worked in Brittany and it was here that he met Gauguin, whose influence is at once recognisable in his work. Prior to painting in Brittany, Bevan had spent some time in Tangier where for one season he had been master of the Tangier Hounds, with Crawhall turning hounds to him. The need to earn a living drove him back to England where he lived for a time on Exmoor, at Hawkridge.

Bevan was, with Sickert, one of the earliest and most influential painters of the Camden Town Group and his best horse pictures were painted from 1911 onwards. He found his inspiration at the London sales run by Tattersall's and Aldridge's where his eye would often be drawn to ex-racehorses who had seen better days and who now, broken down or too old and slow for the racecourse, were sold to end their days as hacks or cab-horses. There is a poignancy and sadness in many of these studies which is often accentuated by the muted colours Bevan used, mainly grey and blue. His use of line is superb, as is his mastery of light and shade, and he was a perceptive observer of the often tawdry urban scene.

Bevan always enjoyed hunting and, after his return from Tangier, hunted at different times with the Crawley and Horsham, the Southdown, the Dulverton and the Devon and Somerset Staghounds. He died in 1925.

In complete contrast to Crawhall and Bevan were Lynwood Palmer and Alfred Grenfell Haigh. Both painted conventional racehorse portraits in the traditional manner, although Palmer often contrived to introduce a romantic element into his portraits. Lynwood Palmer was born in 1868, the third son of a Lincolnshire parson. He was educated at King's College, London but left at the age of seventeen and ran away to Canada rather than face a career in either the law or the diplomatic service. He spent eleven years working on Canadian ranches, sketching whenever time allowed. The turning point in his career came when, accompanying a draft of horses to the United States, he met General Field of the United States Army. The General saw the merit of his sketches and helped him to find work in the United States where he earned his living as an artist for three years.

He returned to England towards the end of the 1890s and, encouraged by the Countess of Warwick, soon found many patrons who wished to have their racehorses, stallions and mares painted. Among the leading racehorses he painted were St Simon, The Tetrarch and Captain Cuttle. His royal patrons included King Edward VII, for whom he painted Minoru, and King George V for whom he painted the filly Scuttle. Many of his pictures were very large, among them *The 6th Duke of Portland's Horses at Welbeck Abbey*, a magnificent painting which measures 66 × 108 in. Palmer's equine portraits were more interesting than those of some of the lesser artists of the time because he frequently incorporated an attractive landscape into the picture. His compositions are sometimes reminiscent of those of Stubbs, although the work is greatly inferior in quality.

A knowledgeable horseman and stud manager, Palmer at one period acted as adviser to Lord Derby. During World War I, in which he was too old to serve in the armed forces, he managed a stud of 750 Royal Mail horses and trained women to drive them. He was a keen whip himself and at times drove a four-in-hand. Despite asthma and poor health, he lived until 1941, although he painted little in his later years.

Alfred Grenfell Haigh was the great-grandson of Daniel Haigh of Tooting, Master of the Surrey Hunt (now the Old Surrey and Burstow) from 1820 to 1836. Daniel was the subject of equestrian portraits by both Abraham Cooper and J. F. Herring, senior. His great-grandson was educated at Rossall and studied in Paris. During World

Lynwood Palmer, *The 6th Duke of Portland's Horses at Welbeck Abbey.*

Alfred Grenfell Haigh, *Mackintosh.*

George Denholm Armour, *The Jockey*.

Cecil Aldin, *The First Open Ditch*.

War I he served with the Lanarkshire Yeomanry.

Haigh started to paint professionally at the turn of the century and went to live at Newmarket where he was soon in demand to paint commissions: among his patrons were the Aga Khan, the Duke of Portland and Lord Rosebery. For many years he painted a succession of top-class racehorses, some of the most notable being The Tetrarch, Bahram, Verdict, Blue Peter, Ocean Swell, Dante and the Grand National winner Shaun Goilin. The last classic winner he painted was the grey, Airborne, winner of the 1946 Derby and St Leger.

Sporting artists are by nature a long-lived breed but Haigh's life was a long one by any standards: he died in his ninety-fourth year. His portraits are accurate, well-painted and attractive. His weakness as an artist was that he contended that it was impossible to portray a horse accurately at the gallop without making it appear unnatural. As a result, his horses never move faster than a fairly sedate trot.

The feeling common among horse painters that the Royal Academy was, and is, prejudiced against their genre is well illustrated by a remark which the retiring master of the Wheatland made on hearing that Haigh's portrait of him had been rejected by the Royal Academy selection committee in 1920: 'If it had been entitled *Nymphs Bathing* it would probably have been accepted!'

In the early years of the century magazines provided employment for scores of artists and illustrators; the advent of the camera has now greatly reduced the demand for this type of work. Two artists who contributed lavishly to the sporting papers of their day were George Denholm Armour (1864–1949) and Cecil Aldin (1870–1935).

The son of a cotton broker, much of Armour's youth was spent in Scotland. He was born in Lanarkshire, went to school in Fife and attended art school in Edinburgh. As a young man he went to Tangier with fellow artist and Scot, Robert Alexander. While there he became a close friend of Joseph Crawhall and the Crawhall influence can be detected in some of his line drawings. On his return to England he took a studio in the Fulham Road and among the periodicals to which he made regular contributions was *Punch*, in which his cartoons appeared for more than thirty years. Many of these cartoons were of racing subjects and they well illustrate the keen observation and pawky sense of humour of their creator.

Like Bevan, he frequented Tattersall's sales and did many drawings of the characters, human and equine, to be seen there. A good horseman and rough rider, Armour also dealt successfully in horses bought at the sales and this form of income helped to pay for his hunting, first with Beaufort and later with the South Berks and Sparkford Vale Harriers. During the war he served, as did many sporting artists, with the Army Remount Service and ended up as Deputy Director of Remounts in Macedonia for which he was awarded the OBE.

Armour was another artist to exceed by a wide margin his three-score years and ten: he died at the age of eighty-five. His autobiography *Bridle and Brush* gives an interesting account of life in England during the first third of this century.

Cecil Aldin's autobiography is also entertaining and has the intriguing title *Time I was Dead* (you must read the book to learn the reason for this). His great strength, in my opinion, lies in his portrayal of dogs rather than racehorses. However, his inclusion in a volume on racing art is justified by his set of four Grand National pictures which were reproduced as a limited edition of prints (*see Plate 3*). He also produced four colour plates and a host of line drawings to illustrate John Masefield's poem *Right Royal*. These pictures are, I feel, easily the best equestrian pictures painted by Aldin and are vastly superior to his rather stiff pictures of hunting countries which were reproduced as prints.

This chapter cannot end without a brief mention of Charlie Johnson Payne (1884–1967), better known as Snaffles, whose prints enjoy perennial popularity. His racing prints are particularly keenly sought and will be well-known to most readers of this book. *The Finest View in Europe* and *The Worst View in Europe* reflect their titles to perfection. However, Snaffles's popularity is more a reflection of his flair for capturing the emotional and nostalgic feeling of his subjects than of the artistic merit of his work.

'Snaffles' (Charlie Johnson Payne), *The Grand National: the Canal Turn.*

TWO

Sir Alfred Munnings

Sir Alfred Munnings stands supreme as the greatest sporting artist of the twentieth century and his only rival for the title of the greatest British sporting artist of all time is George Stubbs (1724–1806). Munnings was the complete painter, equally proficient whether painting landscapes, portraits or animals, and he would have become the leader of his generation in whichever branch of art he had decided to pursue. It is fortunate for admirers of sporting pictures that his love of the countryside and the horse led him to specialise in this branch of art, and his many racing pictures are among the greatest which he produced during his long and fruitful life.

Alfred James Munnings was born at Mendham, Suffolk in October 1878. His parents – his father was a miller and his mother a farmer's daughter – had four sons, of whom he was the second. As with nearly all great artists, he showed an early aptitude for drawing and among his first subjects were his parents, his home at Mendham Mills and, of course, horses. Some of his early work was astonishingly good and, before his fourteenth birthday, he had produced watercolours better than many by trained adult artists.

His formal education was brief and not very happy. After attending a grammar school at Redenhall he was sent to Framlingham College, but this phase of his life lasted only four terms and, at the age of fourteen, he was sent to Page Bros and Co., in Norwich, to start a six-year apprenticeship as a lithographer. Although the hours which the firm demanded from its apprentices were long, the young Munnings never-theless found time most evenings to put in a couple of hours at the Norwich School of Art where he learned watercolour painting. Success in this medium soon came his way and his work was accepted for exhibition by the Royal Institute of Watercolour Artists while he was still a teenager.

Growing up in Norwich, Munnings, like all painters of the Norwich School, soon became proficient at reproducing on canvas those massive skies which dominate the landscape near the Norfolk coast. In his later work he was able to use his impressive skies to complement whatever landscape was required in his paintings.

At this time he received much valuable help and criticism from James Reeve, the leading authority on the Norwich School of painters and curator of the Castle Museum and Art Gallery. Reeve, a splendid Dickensian figure with grey sidewhiskers, also introduced Munnings to cigar smoking and continued to help him after Munnings left Norwich by commissioning a watercolour for the Art Gallery and then buying an oil. The latter, measuring thirty inches by fifty inches, was of an old countryman leading a mare and foal by a blossoming elder bush and for it the young artist received eighty-five pounds, a vast fortune to him.

Munnings was not yet out of his apprenticeship when, in 1899, his first two paintings were accepted by the Royal Academy. Both were river scenes, the first of two children in a boat and the second of his friend 'Jumbo' Betts fishing for pike from the river bank on a cold winter afternoon. These were the first of nearly three hundred pictures shown at the Royal Academy during his lifetime. The day when news arrived of the acceptance by the Royal Academy of these two pictures was described by Munnings in *An Artist's Life* as 'the greatest day of my life'. To celebrate he went with a friend, Ralph Wernham, by train to Bungay races; the sights which he saw that day were to influence the rest of his life and work:

> There were roundabouts, shooting-galleries, swinging-boats and coconut shies; large eating-and drinking-tents, flags flying, and thousands of oranges blazing on stalls in the sun. I had never seen such droves of ponies and gypsy lads. But all this, with music and noise, died away and dwindled to nothing when I saw the Thoroughbred horses and jockeys – professional and gentleman riders (riding with a proper length, and not with the short leathers of to-day) – in bright silk colours, going off down the course.*

Munning's genius as an artist is all the more remarkable because he suffered from two physical handicaps. At the age of twenty, while he was lifting a foxhound puppy over a fence, a twig sprang back and blinded him in his right eye. A severe enough handicap to anyone, this was a particularly cruel blow to an artist to whom the use of both eyes is generally considered essential in order to obtain a correct sense of perspective. Ten years later, Munnings suffered his first attack of gout, that painful and recurrent complaint which was eventually to end his painting career.

On leaving Page Bros, Munnings established himself at Mendham, using an old carpenter's shop as a studio, and painted mainly Norfolk scenes. He also attended Frank Calderon's summer school of animal painting at Finchingfield in Essex. His artistic and social horizons were further widened when he was taken abroad by Shaw Tomkins, a director of Caley's Chocolates, for whom Munnings had produced posters while

*Sir Alfred Munnings, *An Artist's Life*.

Sir Alfred Munnings, *The Start at Newmarket*, detail.

an apprentice. He attended Julian's in Paris, his first visit being in 1904, where he was able to study figure painting and to meet many of his artistic contemporaries. While in Paris he visited all the major galleries and was at once delighted and inspired by the fresh approach of the Impressionists. From them he acquired the habit of using light and shade to bring life to his pictures and this technique, allied to his bold use of colour, was to become one of the main features of his work.

This mention of colour leads me to the three volumes of autobiography which Munnings wrote, *An Artist's Life, The Second Burst* and *The Finish*. These books, published in the early 1950s, give a fascinating picture of life in the first half of this century. They also tell us a great deal about the author, who saw life in exciting colours in the way that musicians or poets hear life in terms of sound. His delightful reminiscences sparkle with vitality and skip from one subject to another, from one period to another, with the unpredictability of a grasshopper. The books also contain nearly five hundred illustrations of the artist's work.

While in his twenties Munnings started to hunt, a recreation which gave him not only great pleasure but also an essential insight into the people and horses who were to become his subjects and his livelihood. He hunted first with the Norwich Staghounds and the Dunston Harriers and later with Mr Bolitho's hounds in Cornwall. He was lured down to Cornwall by his desire to visit the famous artists' colony at Newlyn and he formed lasting friendships with several members of the Newlyn School, among them Augustus John, Lamorna Birch and Harold and Laura Knight. Munnings himself set up a studio at Lamorna and spent part of each year from 1910 until the outbreak of World War I in Cornwall. Some of his best work at this time was done on the moor near Zennor and on the forbidding granite-strewn slopes of Zennor Hill.

The other great influence on the artist's life prior to 1914 was that of the gypsies. Every year some two or three hundred of these travelling people would migrate to Alton in Hampshire for the hop-picking and Munnings would follow them. They proved splendid models, the women posing in their best clothes and most extravagant hats and receiving the same rate of pay for modelling as they would have received for the more arduous work of hop-picking. Munnings revelled in the life and colour which emanated from the gypsy encampments and the caravans, horses, lurchers, swarthy men and gaily attired women inspired him to paint pictures which many of his critics consider to be among his finest. Later in life he was to return to gypsy subjects and he painted many pictures, some reproduced as prints, of gypsies on Epsom Downs where they congregated for the Derby meeting.

When war broke out in 1914, Munnings made several attempts to enlist in the army but was graded C3 and rejected because of the blindness in his right eye. However, his persistence paid off when he wrote to his fellow artist Cecil Aldin, a major in command of a Remount depot near Reading. Aldin summoned Munnings to Calcot Park, then the home of Canadian artillery horses, and Munnings became an expert in the treatment of lice and mange in horses.

Much later in the war Munnings succeeded in reaching France, not as a soldier but as an official war artist attached to the Canadian Cavalry Brigade under General Seely. He was in France during 1917–18 and produced a host of sketches, portraits and canvases, so that, on his return to London, even Paul Konody, the art critic of the *Observer*, was impressed by the size and range of his output. Konody had been given the job by the Canadian Government of selecting artists to go out to France to paint scenes of the war and, in 1919, the Royal Academy put on the Canadian War Records Exhibition. Forty of the pictures in this exhibition were by Munnings.

The inter-war years saw Munnings in ever-increasing demand to paint racing and hunting commissions for some of the leading owners and sportsmen of the period. He had painted his first famous racehorse, the Grand National winner Poethlyn, in 1919, but now commissions came thick and fast. As with many popular artists before and since, he painted too much and at times felt overwhelmed by the amount of work he took on. Nor was it all plain sailing, despite the freedom and surety of line which appear in his work. As he wrote, 'The difficulties and troubles of horse painting are a hundredfold.'

The year 1919 was something of an *annus mirabilis* for him. The Canadian War Records Exhibition established his reputation; he was elected an Associate of the Royal Academy; he rented, in Glebe Place, Chelsea, his first London Studio; he bought Castle House at Dedham, in Constable country, for £1,800 and he met the woman who was, the following spring, to become his second wife. His first, the artist Florence Carter-Wood, had committed suicide during the second year of their marriage.

Violet McBride, a young widow, was the daughter of a riding master and it was at Richmond Horse Show that she first caught Munnings's eye. An elegant rider, she acted as model for her husband on many occasions and also took over the running of his business affairs, leaving him free to pursue his art unencumbered with financial worry. In addition, she accepted his long absences from home, whether he was staying in the country with patrons or in London, where his love of good companionship drew him to the Chelsea Arts Club and the Garrick.

Among the racehorse commissions painted between the wars were Bahram, Book Law, Coronach, Hyperion, Mahmoud, Mr Jinks, Son-in-Law, Brown Jack, Humorist, Solario and Tiberius, the four last-named being reproduced as prints. Munnings's race-horse portraits all succeeded in bringing his subjects to life in a way which nineteenth century artists never achieved. He also conveyed the fact that the thoroughbred is a highly-strung, vital creature bred for racing. His technique here was to depict movement, however slight, in the posed portrait by showing the horse with a raised foreleg, an ear back, playing with the bit or showing 'the look of eagles'. Where the horse is held by a lad, he captures the rapport between the two and the portrait invariably contains features of interest other than the main subject. He brought into play his skill as a landscape painter, whether painting mares and foals in tree-lined paddocks, horses on the racecourse or scenes in the stableyard or on the gallops. In all his racing works the marvellous skies, a legacy from his Norwich days, complete the picture.

His visits to the racecourse gave him particular pleasure and resulted in many memorable paintings. Epsom provided him with a bonus in that he had not only the racing but also his gypsies. Three of his best Epsom pictures were reproduced as prints, *The Paddock at the Spring Meeting, Unsaddling at the Summer Meeting* and *Going Out at Epsom*, for which picture his own horses Chips and Kaffir were the models and his man Slocombe the jockey.

An unusual racing picture was *Their Majesties Return from Ascot, 1925,* painted at Queen Mary's suggestion, which shows Her Majesty and King George V returning to Windsor Castle in their open carriage drawn by four greys. Munnings loved greys and tried whenever possible to have one in his stables as a model. The almost white pony Augereau appeared in many of his early pictures.

On occasions the horses which Munnings was asked to paint would come to live in his yard, a case of the mountain coming to Mahomet. Brown Jack was one such and the artist came to know him particularly well because he had the gallant gelding in his stables for six weeks while he made a model of him for the bronze statue which was commissioned by the Jockey Club. This was one of the very few bronzes which Munnings did. Oils were his favourite medium and although his watercolours are often excellent they cannot capture the richness, texture and depth which make his oil paintings so superb.

Munnings and his wife continued to hunt whenever they could although they gave contrasting performances in the saddle, as described by John Skeaping in *Drawn From Life*. Skeaping whipped in to the Essex and Suffolk in the 'thirties and the Munningses were regular followers. 'Sir Alfred looked like a sack of potatoes when mounted on his thoroughbreds, over-fat because they didn't get enough exercise at the slow pace at which he jogged along. He was too insecure to go any faster. On the other hand, Lady Munnings was a first-class horsewoman and looked wonderful riding side-saddle, taking any obstacle that presented itself.'

There is food for serious thought here because I and many far better judges – among them Lionel Edwards – have often felt that some of Munnings's beautifully painted hunters look as if they have never done a day's hunting. Similarly some of the colts and geldings appearing in his racing pictures have necks and crests on them which

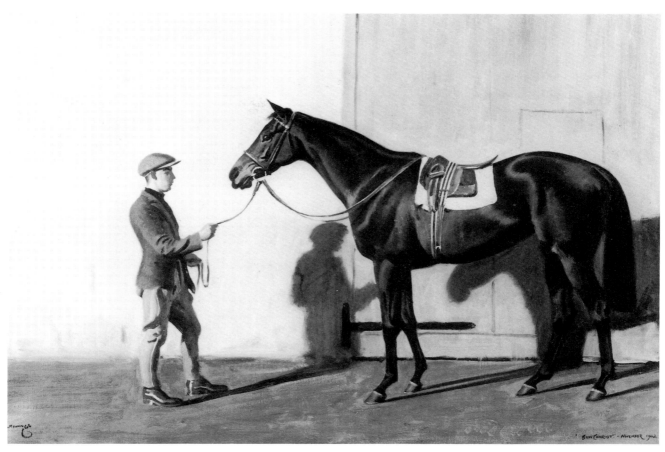

Sir Alfred Munnings, *Sun Chariot*.

Sir Alfred Munnings, *In the Saddling Paddock, Cheltenham, March Meeting*.

would do justice to a mature stallion. Could it be that he relied too heavily on his 'over-fat thoroughbred' as models?

When World War II broke out Castle House was taken over by the army and the Munningses moved down to Withypool to find on Exmoor that happiness and inspiration which other artists have so often found there. The income from commissions painted during the previous twenty years – allied to his wife's keen business sense – had made him financially secure and he was able to re-emerge as the true countryman he had always been. Many of the pictures painted at this time were Exmoor landscapes.

In 1944 Munnings received the supreme accolade from his fellow artists by being elected President of the Royal Academy. He beat Augustus John, his old friend from pre-World War I days in Cornwall, by twenty-four votes to eleven. He was the first sporting painter this century to be elected President and it is long odds against another sporting artist filling this role during the next fifty years. Predictably, his presidency was not a success. He was no diplomat, no administrator, quick tempered and disinclined to listen to views other than his own ultra-conservative ones. His infamous speech at the Royal Academy Banquet on 18 April 1949, in which he succeeded in offending almost everyone who in any way broke with tradition, saw the nadir of his popularity and he resigned at the end of the year.

In the 'fifties he continued to paint and was surprised and delighted when his three volumes of autobiography received rapturous acclaim from critics and readers, by no means all of whom were interested in horses and art. He made several visits to Newmarket, painting *Before the Start*, *October Meeting* and *Warren Hill* and he painted one of his best steeplechasing pictures, *In the Saddling Paddock, Cheltenham March Meeting*. He also painted racing portraits, though fewer in number than before. The last of these was of HM The Queen's Aureole who finished second in the 1953 Derby to Pinza, on whom Sir Gordon Richards achieved his sole, long-awaited, Derby victory.

In 1956 the Royal Academy gave him a retrospective exhibition at Burlington House, thus showing that most of the wounds caused during his presidency had been healed. He had achieved much in his lifetime – he had also been knighted and had become a Freeman of the City of Norwich – and he undoubtedly enjoyed to the full the opportunities which his talent had brought his way. In his declining years he was increasingly plagued by gout and heart trouble and he died in his sleep on 17 July 1959, aged eighty.

Although successful in portraying little equine movements, he never captured the speed of horses racing in the way that Holiday, Skeaping or Curling have – but then, he never attempted to. Despite this possible chink in his armour he remains unquestionably the greatest racing painter of this century, an opinion shared by critics, dealers and collectors who pay large sums for his pictures. For those of us who cannot afford to buy these pictures, the alternative is to visit his old home, Castle House, Dedham, which is now a museum dedicated to his life and work.

Sir Alfred Munnings, *Saucy Sue winning The Oaks, 1925.*

THREE

Lionel Edwards

Hunting was the first love of Lionel Edwards's life. In the words of that well-known foxhunter and writer 'Bay' de Courcy Parry: 'Lionel Edwards was not just a great painter who went hunting; he was rather a great hunting man who painted wonderful pictures.' By his own admission, Edwards put hunting before all else, for he used to say: 'In 1902 two very important events occurred – I had my first real staghunting and I got engaged to Ethel.' Friends used to suggest to him that the order should perhaps be reversed, but no such reversal was made.

National Hunt racing appealed to Edwards because of its close relationship with hunting but he could never drum up much enthusiasm for flat racing, much as he loved and admired the horses involved. Nevertheless, Edwards must rank as one of the foremost racing painters of the century because he brought to his racing pictures the same understanding and skills which made him the supreme hunting artist. In particular he could convey better than any of his contemporaries the muted colours and dampness of our British winter landscape.

This feeling of authenticity which pervades his hunting pictures comes through again in his steeplechasing scenes. Those who have ridden in races can stand in front of many of Edwards's best steeplechasing pictures and, with no great effort of imagination, recall the reins made slippery by rain and sweat, the creak of leather, the sound of hooves on sodden turf and the flying clods of mud. His summer pictures of flat racing lack the same feeling of involvement and this is because of his own lack of interest in the subject. Munnings, for example, was much more successful in capturing the colour, the glamour and the excitement of a flat race meeting in June.

Lionel Edwards's great love of hunting was inherited from his father, Dr James Edwards, who practised in Chester. Dr Edwards's first wife died when he was only thirty-five and, soon after her death, he gave up his practice and bought Benarth Hall and its run-down estate near Conway, in North Wales. He married again but his second wife died in childbirth. Each winter, Dr Edwards would travel to Leamington to hunt

Alfred Grenfell Haigh, *Dilerjung and William Rufus with their syce on a racecourse.*

PLATE 3

Cecil Aldin, *The Canal Turn.*

Sir Alfred Munnings, *Study No 4 for A Start at Newmarket.*

PLATE 4

Sir Alfred Munnings, *A Park Meeting: The Eclipse Stakes, Sandown.*

Sir Alfred Munnings, *Mon Talisman at Chantilly (H. Semblat)* (detail).

PLATE 5

Lionel Edwards, *Epsom: The Oaks, 1949.*

PLATE 6

Lionel Edwards, *A Trial on the Limekilns, Newmarket.*

Lionel Edwards, *The Water Jump, Cheltenham*.

Lionel Edwards, *December Meeting, Cheltenham*.

Lionel Edwards, *Going Out, Newmarket*.

Lionel Edwards, *The Start, Goodwood*.

with the Warwickshire, leaving Mary Jane, the only surviving child of his first two marriages, at Benarth.

Mary Jane grew understandably lonely and Dr Edwards brought Harriet Main, a cousin of his first wife, down from Kelso to act as companion to his daughter. As so often happens, propinquity turned out to be the father of romance and the doctor duly married Harriet. He was in his late forties; she was two years younger than his daughter. The marriage proved not only harmonious but fruitful. Harriet produced five sons, of whom Lionel, born in Clifton in 1878, was the last. His father, who had been born five years before the battle of Waterloo, died when Lionel was seven.

Young Lionel spent a happy childhood at Benarth. His brothers were away in the army or at school and there was little money available for his education, which was sporadic and informal. He lived in a world of adults and animals and, from the age of five onwards, showed a marked talent for drawing. In this he was following in the footsteps of Frank, the fourth of the five brothers. Frank attended the Hubert Herkomer School but died of cholera at the age of twenty while staying with Fitz, the eldest of the five, in India. Lionel seemed at first destined to follow Fitz into the army and was sent to a crammer with this end in view. However, he showed little inclination towards the practice of soldiering, although he liked the theory. Asked to leave the crammer, he then went to Frank Calderon's School of Animal Painting in Baker Street. He left Frank Calderon at the age of twenty-one, having won a couple of scholarships and, for the next six years, had a studio in London in Holland Street. In 1898, at the age of twenty, he became the youngest member of the London Sketch Club and here he met many artists, among them Cecil Aldin, John Hassall and Phil May.

In 1905, Lionel Edwards married Ethel Ashness Wells. She was the daughter of a retired director of a brewing firm and the young couple had known each other for several years before their marriage. Ethel shared her husband's love of horses and the countryside and she proved a marvellous wife during their long and happy marriage. She usually remained at home while he went off on his several painting expeditions. Whenever invited to paint a hunting commission he would, if at all possible, fit in at least one day's sport with the pack concerned; his trips to Ireland gave him particular pleasure. One of the few trips which the Edwardses made together was to Gibraltar in 1929. Among the pictures painted during this visit were two very interesting watercolours, *The Royal Calpe Point-to-Point Meeting* and *Racing at Gibraltar (on the North Front)*. Both were reproduced as prints and these prints are very rare.

Lionel and Ethel Edwards spent their honeymoon on Exmoor and she was at once captivated by this beautiful part of England which has proved an inspiration for so many artists. The Edwardses had five children: Derrick, Philip, Marjorie, Lindsay and Kenneth. Marjorie has inherited her father's facility with the pen – her *Figures in a*

Landscape is a fascinating reminiscence of the artist and his family – while Lindsay, who sadly died in 1987, inherited a considerable measure of the old man's skill as a watercolourist.

When World War I broke out, Edwards joined the Army Remount Service and spent the greater part of his four years in uniform at the Remount depot near Romsey in Hampshire. The job at Romsey consisted of taking in horses purchased by the army and fitting them for service overseas as heavy draught horses, light draught gunners, officers' chargers or cavalry troop horses. As a break in the monotonous routine of life at the depot, Edwards would sometimes accompany a draft of horses across the Channel for delivery to the fighting units.

Not long after demobilisation, Edwards, while hunting with the Hursley, spotted a Victorian house twelve miles from Salisbury on the Hampshire Downs. This house, Buckholt, was to become home for him and his family for the rest of his life.

Most of Edwards's best work was produced between the two World Wars. During the 'twenties he was commissioned to paint a set of racehorses for the *Illustrated Sporting and Dramatic News* for reproduction as prints. This set included the flying grey The Tetrarch, Epinard and Lord Derby's 1924 Derby winner Sansovino. Edwards's hunting prints are almost legion but his racing prints are fewer in number and greatly sought after. I particularly like the Newmarket prints published by The Sporting Gallery; these four, entitled *Morning Exercise, A Training Gallop, The Ditch* and *Warren Hill*, give a very good impression of Newmarket between the wars and the canvas of Warren Hill was considered by the artist to be one of the best he ever painted.

The role of the artist as the recorder of contemporary dress and customs is an important one, although less so since the invention of the camera. In this connexion, Edwards's pictures of point-to-points between the wars are of great interest, particularly to those present-day enthusiasts who are too young to remember the days when point-to-point riders wore hunting clothes.

Many of Edwards's best racing pictures were painted as illustrations for books. He collaborated with Bob Lyle, the racing correspondent of *The Times*, by producing the illustrations for *Brown Jack* and *The Aga Khan's Horses*. The pencil drawings in the former are particularly good. After the favourable reception of these books, Edwards suggested to Lyle that the latter should write a history of Royal Newmarket; the artist had always had a keen interest in history, and it was this aspect of Newmarket rather than the purely racing angle which prompted him to make his suggestion. The book was due for publication in 1940 but, because of the war, its appearance was postponed until 1945. In the meantime Bob Lyle had died and the book was finished by Adair Dighton. *Royal Newmarket* contains some very good racing pictures, as well as portraits of the classic winners Big Game and Sun Chariot, bred by the National Stud and raced

Lionel Edwards, *The Start, Doncaster*.

Lionel Edwards, *The Bend, Two Mile Steeplechase, Cheltenham*.

Lionel Edwards, *1923 Grand National: Becher's Brook,*
Sergeant Murphy and Captain Bennett.

by King George VI, who between them won four of the 1942 classics.

In addition to illustrating twenty-five of his own books, Edwards illustrated books for more than fifty other authors. One of his happiest associations was with the poet Will Ogilvie, who lived near Selkirk, in the Borders, and for whom Edwards illustrated five volumes of sporting verse. Among my favourite lines from Ogilvie's racing poems are the last two verses of 'Aintree Calls!'

> *Ghosts of men that here have ridden*
> *Gather at the post unbidden,*
> > *Waiting till the old flag falls;*
> *Hear the rattled guard-rails quiver*
> *As they rush them, game as ever!*
> *(Mist, O mist, on Mersey River!)*
> > *Aintree calls!*
>
> *Danger beckons yet to daring,*
> *And the colours wait for wearing,*
> *While Fame proffers gifts for sharing*
> > *And Dame Fortune plans the falls.*
> *Lo! The spirit of endeavour*
> *Burns in England's heart for ever;*
> > *Aintree calls!*

Edwards made several trips to Aintree and among the good pictures he painted of those massive fences, which in his day were even more fearsome than they are today, is one of the 1923 Grand National winner, Sergeant Murphy, leading over Becher's.

Another whose work he illustrated was Adam Lindsay Gordon, a poet who had no peer when it came to conveying the atmosphere and excitement of the racecourse. In 'How We Beat the Favourite', Gordon succinctly describes the perennial problem of qualifying point-to-pointers:

> *He calls hunted fairly, a horse that has barely*
> *Been stripped for a trot within sight of the hounds*

and his immortal lines from '*In Utrumque Paratus*' should be the motto of all spirited youth:

> *No game was ever yet worth a rap for a rational man to play*
> *Into which no accident, no mishap, could possibly find its way.*

In view of his interest in history, Edwards must have derived particular pleasure from *British Racecourses* which he illustrated for Bill Curling, who was the *Daily*

Lionel Edwards, *Mare and Foals in a Paddock at Clanville Lodge*.

Telegraph's racing correspondent 'Hotspur'. This book was published in 1951, when Edwards was seventy-three, and the twelve watercolours which he produced for it show how well he retained his powers in old age.

Motoring was a great pleasure to Edwards throughout his life. This was just as well, given the amount of travelling which he had to undertake in the course of his work. He never learned to drive a car but would sit beside the chauffeur, who towards the end of his life was often one of his sons, Lindsay or Kenneth, and enjoy the countryside. He had an unnerving habit, when there was a passenger in the back, of turning round suddenly, right arm extended, to point out some feature of the landscape. This display of enthusiasm caused several minor accidents and the job of chauffeur to 'the Maestro', as Peter Biegel called him, was always an exciting one. Indeed, it is his love of the British landscape in all weathers that comes through in all his most important work.

A useful rule-of-thumb for a sporting picture is to remove the main subject and then see what remains. In too many pictures by the younger generation, the answer is 'precious little'. The pictures of Edwards and Munnings stand up to this test probably better than the work of any other sporting artists of this century. Both were marvellous landscape painters.

Although Edwards painted many racehorse portraits, his forte was the action picture and he was more fluent in watercolour and gouache than in oils. When painting portraits, his depiction of the human figure seldom reached the high standard of his equine portraits. In addition to those horses already mentioned, he painted the 1941 Derby winner Owen Tudor and in 1949 he painted the Hon. Dorothy Paget's Straight Deal, six years after his Epsom triumph.

Edwards continued to paint regularly until his death in 1966. In the previous year he had travelled by air to Ireland with his daughter Marjorie to paint Charlottesville and Petite Etoile for the Aga Khan. It was the first occasion on which he had flown and he considered it a very dull method of travel because he could see little of the countryside. Mercifully he was not allowed to sit beside the pilot.

Lionel Edwards always maintained that his brother artists took themselves too seriously and he was scornful of 'the artistic temperament', considering it to be an excuse for behaviour which would not be tolerated in other people. He wrote two autobiographical volumes, *Scarlet and Corduroy* (1941) and *Reminiscences of a Sporting Artist* (1947), and his modesty and love of nature are at once evident to the readers of these books. During his long life he gave enormous pleasure to the many friends he made in all walks of life. The seal on his greatness as an artist was set in 1986 when the British Sporting Art Trust mounted a superb exhibition of his work and this work will continue to give pleasure to succeeding generations.

FOUR

Gilbert Holiday

Of those artists born in the nineteenth century, the one most successful in portraying the sheer speed of horses racing was Gilbert Holiday. He was considered by many fine judges, among them Lionel Edwards, to be the first artist to make use of the revelations of the camera. He depicted horses in action in the manner to which we are now accustomed but which at the beginning of this century seemed revolutionary to those used to the 'rocking-horse gallop' as depicted by artists from the seventeenth century onwards.

Edwards was to say in the 1940s that 'Holiday, by clever manipulation of dust or mud and the consequent blurring of outlines, was able to give a tremendous sense of speed. When handling a mass of horsemen he was even better, and he would use even the most grotesque positions with success.'* In this he initiated a technique which was to be continued and refined in the second half of the century by such as John Skeaping and Peter Curling.

Charles Gilbert Joseph Holiday was born in Maida Vale on 29 January 1879, a year later than Munnings and Edwards. He chose to be called by his middle Christian name, although to many of his friends and admirers he was always 'G H' and it was with these initials that many of his pictures were signed. He was the second son of Frederick Charles Holiday, a distinguished civil servant who was knighted on his retirement from the India Office and who then went to live with his family at Whitwell, near Hitchin.

Although Holiday's mother, Adela Maria Mileham, was a competent amateur water-colourist, the most artistically gifted member of his family was his uncle Henry Holiday (1839–1927). Henry was friendly with several of the Pre-Raphaelites, notably Holman Hunt and Burne-Jones, and his masterpiece is probably *Dante and Beatrice* which now hangs in the Walker Art Gallery, Liverpool.

After attending Warwick House School at Maida Hill, Holiday moved on at the age

*Lionel Edwards, *Reminiscences of a Sporting Artist*

Gilbert Holiday, *Self-Portrait, c*1903–4.

of thirteen to Westminster. Here his artistic talent did not escape the notice of his housemaster, Mr Ralph Tanner, who used to award Holiday an unusual punishment when his Latin prose work failed to reach the required standard. Instead of asking his pupil to write the piece out again, Tanner would say: 'Bring me six horses' heads by tomorrow morning'. In this way, Tanner's collection grew rapidly and he could, I suppose, be regarded as the first collector of Holiday's work.

On leaving Westminster, Holiday entered the Royal Academy Schools and was soon influenced by the daring approach of the Impressionists so that, rather than relying on line, he chose to use the contrast of light and shade to achieve the atmosphere and movement which were to become the hallmarks of his work. He had a broad and direct method of working and frequently mixed his media.

As with so many artists of his generation, he first started to earn his living as an illustrator for magazines, his earliest work appearing in *The Strand Magazine* and *The Graphic* in 1900. It is a sad fact of life for artists that they are seldom required in this role nowadays, their function having been usurped by photographers.

Holiday's work at this time was mostly in black and white and it was in this medium, later to be abandoned, that he first made his name. Indeed it was thanks to his black and white illustrations for *The Graphic* that he was able to get married. He had been engaged for some time to Mina Marguerite Spencer of Guernsey but it was not until he received a contract to produce a weekly page for this journal that the young couple felt financially secure enough to marry. This they did in Guernsey in 1908.

The only known self-portrait of Holiday dates from the time of his engagement (*see page 43*). He sent it to his fiancée and she, a girl of outstanding good looks, used to joke that he had flattered the sitter. Holiday's life was not a long one; his wife survived him by more than forty years, dying in 1982 in her ninety-ninth year. After their wedding, the Holidays rented a flat in Albany Mansions, Battersea. He also had a studio in Chelsea and was a member of the Langham Sketch Club.

Although kept busy with his illustrative work in the decade leading up to the outbreak of World War I, Holiday also found time for more serious painting. His interest in horses took him to Olympia where he executed several oil sketches behind the scenes, including many sketches of farriers at work. His first Royal Academy picture, *The Brewer's Dray*, was accepted in 1904 and four of his six Academy pictures date from this decade, the last two being hunting subjects. His favourite themes at this time were the hunting field and artillery gun teams in action. He spent as much time as he could with the Gunners and it was in portraying the speed and excitement of the gun teams manoeuvring that, in the opinion of his friend 'Snaffles', he reached his zenith as an artist. This opinion is not universally shared, many considering his racing pictures to be paramount.

Gilbert Holiday, *Ascot*.

Shortly after the declaration of war in August 1914 Holiday went out to the front as an unofficial war artist. Dressed in civilian clothes and sketching wherever he went, he not unnaturally attracted the attention of the military authorities and quickly recorded an unusual – and unenviable – double. Within a short time he was arrested as a spy by both the British and the French. Although he soon convinced the British of his innocence, the French were less easily persuaded and he was sentenced to death by firing squad. He was saved in the nick of time by a French officer with whom he had earlier become friendly.

Sharing in the patriotic fervour which swept England at the outset of the war, Holiday determined to join the army at all costs. At that stage men over thirty were considered too old for enlistment but Holiday succeeded in obtaining a commission in the Royal Field Artillery in 1915 by falsifying his age: he was in fact thirty-five. When Holiday returned to France he was made a Forward Observation Officer, an example of a round peg being fitted into a round hole. The most hazardous part of his job as F O O was to remain in No Man's Land sketching the enemy-held landscape during the hours of daylight. He would then withdraw under cover of darkness to his dugout where he worked his sketches up into detailed maps of the enemy lines. These maps were then used for the laying of our guns.

Although mercifully he did not suffer the dangers and privations undergone by such as the poets Siegfried Sassoon, Robert Graves or Wilfred Owen, nevertheless his army service was not without its share of danger and unpleasantness. On one occasion he was pursued and machine-gunned by a German aircraft while returning to the British lines from one of his sketching stints. On another he was buried in a cellar while finishing one of his maps. His life was saved in this instance by a large cupboard which fell across him and protected him from the falling masonry. The demolition of the building by enemy shell fire was so complete that it was assumed that Holiday must have perished and a report of his death was sent to his family. After he – and the providential cupboard – had been dug out of the rubble the report was fortunately intercepted before it reached its destination.

Holiday remained in the war zone from 1915 to 1918 and was present at the battles of Ypres, Arras and Passchendaele. Some of his most evocative work was carried out in 1917 during the third battle of Ypres. He sketched whenever he was able and his many sketches, drawings and paintings provide a faithful and valuable record of this most horrific of European wars. The Imperial War Museum contains five of Holiday's pictures. The largest is his painting of the ruined Square and Cloth Hall at Ypres and he also painted the 'Ubique' set, a series of four paintings showing artillery life in Flanders. He remained with the Army of Occupation in Germany until he left the army in 1919 and perhaps his most important painting of this period was that of General Plumer taking the salute under the statue of the Kaiser as the 19th Division entered Cologne over the Hohenzollern Bridge. This picture was shown at the Royal Academy in 1919. He was also one of the principal artists whose work was included in the *Royal Artillery War Commemoration Book*, (1920), 'The Gunner Bible'.

On demobilisation Holiday resumed his happy family life with his wife and two daughters, Climene and Mary, who had by now gone to live near East Molesey in Surrey. Together they enjoyed many holidays in Guernsey where he produced several pictures of life on the island. Among the most attractive of these were various pictures of horses, and sometimes even oxen, hauling laden carts up from the beaches during the seaweed harvest.

For the last fifteen years of his life Holiday concentrated for the most part on sporting subjects and it is these pictures which have the greatest appeal to the majority of today's collectors. He spent much time on the racecourse, painting pictures of Ascot, Sandown,

Gilbert Holiday, *Captain Bennett and Turkey Buzzard fall
at Becher's, 1921 Grand National.*

Goodwood, Liverpool and many other courses. After a visit to Ireland he produced a set of pictures, published as prints in 1929, of racing over the famous banks at Punchestown. Another set of his racing pictures to be printed was of the Aintree fences. These Punchestown and Liverpool pictures are among the best examples of his work, showing his Impressionist use of light and colour to capture atmosphere. In one of the Liverpool pictures, *A Fall at the [Canal] Turn*, he used a favourite trick, that of painting horses from behind.

One of the techniques which set Holiday apart from other artists of his period was this love of painting horses from unusual angles. In his superb *Epsom – Rounding Tattenham Corner in the Derby*, he shows the leaders' hindquarters while the main body of the field is seen, more conventionally, from the side (*see Plate 10*). Again the artist has placed himself behind his subjects in *At the End of the Rainbow – A Crock of Gold For Someone – A Sandown Park Impression* (*see Plate 8*). Both pictures provide excellent examples of his daring use of colour and of the way in which he used different media – in these instances watercolour and pastel – to create the impression which he required.

One of my favourite Holiday pictures, a pastel of nostalgic charm, is *Racehorses arriving at Hampton Court for Hurst Park Races*. During the 'twenties and 'thirties the train was, of course, not only the most common form of transport for racehorses but also on occasions conveyed hunters and hounds to the meet and home again after a day's hunting.

Holiday painted few formal racehorse portraits, his great talent lying in capturing the atmosphere and movement of the racecourse, but on occasions his action racing pictures were of named horses and incidents. A good example of this type of picture is his painting of Turkey Buzzard falling in front of Shaun Spadah and The Bore at Becher's in the 1921 Grand National.

His years as a Gunner left a great impression on Holiday and many of the figures in his pictures were men of distinctly military mien, with square jaws and neatly trimmed moustaches. This description fitted Holiday himself and another of his tricks was to place himself in the foreground of some of his pictures. He can be recognised, invariably wearing his distinctive grey trilby with its broad black band, leaning on the rails at Ascot, standing beside Becher's or watching a game of polo.

Although the best equestrian artists are said to be at home in the saddle, this remark was even more true of Holiday than of the others because he had the unusual habit of sitting in a saddle, placed at a convenient height, while painting in his studio. He enjoyed hunting and, during a check, would frequently whip a scrap of paper from his pocket to make a sketch which would later be worked up into a complete picture in the studio. Hunting was indirectly responsible for his death. In 1932, while hunting

Lionel Edwards, *In the Paddock, Cheltenham March Meeting.*

PLATE 7

Lionel Edwards, *The Bibury Cup, Salisbury 1933.*

Gilbert Holiday, *At the End of the Rainbow – A Crock of Gold for Someone – A Sandown Park Impression.*

Gilbert Holiday, *'There Goes Your Shirt'.*

PLATE 8

with the Woolwich Drag, he had a bad fall over timber, crushing his spinal cord. He was paralysed from the waist down and spent the remaining five years of his life in a wheelchair. Nevertheless, with his customary cheerful courage, he continued to sketch and paint, and during this period of confinement he wrote and illustrated *We'll All Go a'Hunting Today*.

During the winter of 1936 Holiday caught a bad cold which developed first into bronchitis and then into pneumonia. He died three weeks before his fifty-eighth birthday and was buried close to his parents at Whitwell in Hertfordshire. Holiday's paralysing accident and premature death were tragic because, artists being a late-maturing breed, he was only reaching his peak at the time of his horrific fall. During his lifetime he never had a one-man exhibition, most of his pictures being commissions for individuals or magazines. His pictures rarely come on to the open market and it was not until 1983 that the public had the opportunity to make a full appraisal of his work. In that year William Marler, the Shropshire dealer who had been collecting his work for several years, put on a retrospective exhibition at the Tryon Gallery in London. Since then the public appetite for Holiday's work has increased voraciously and he ranks with Munnings and Edwards as one of the three great equestrian artists of the first half of this century.

Gilbert Holiday, *Racehorses unloading at Hampton Court for Hurst Park Races.*

John Skeaping, *The Finish*.

FIVE

John Skeaping

John Skeaping's place in twentieth century racing art is unique in that he is the only artist who reached the top rank both as a painter and a sculptor. Having said that, there is no doubt that Munnings would also have excelled in both fields had he chosen to sculpt more than the three bronzes which he completed.

Skeaping's initial training was as a direct carver (i.e., one who creates his model from a single block of stone, marble, wood or other material) and it was only in middle age that he started to paint the racing scene. He became a prolific painter and his forte was to capture the movement and speed of the racehorse. However it is as a sculptor that he is chiefly remembered and he remains, at the time of writing, the leading equine sculptor of the century.

John Rattenbury Skeaping was born on 9 June 1901 in South Woodford, Essex. His father was a portrait painter who had, in his youth, lived in Paris and shared a studio with Cézanne; his mother was a music teacher. His parents were devoted to each other and to their four children, of whom John was the third.

The Skeaping home was unconventional in the extreme. Both his parents were totally unworldly and his mother was the reverse of house-proud – to such an extent that the young John was encouraged to draw with charcoal all over the white-washed walls of the home as soon as his talent for drawing became evident.

None of the four Skeaping children was sent to school, their father having no belief in 'general education'. He would have enjoyed Bernard Shaw's view of education: 'casting artificial pearls before real swine'. What Skeaping's father did believe in, however, was a basic training in the arts and this his children received, to the exclusion of all else. They would be taken by their father to the London galleries and museums and by their mother to concerts, the theatre and the ballet. Dancing made the most profound impression on the young John and one of his most lasting childhood memories was of a visit to the Diaghilev Ballet when he was about ten years old.

At the age of thirteen Skeaping enrolled at Blackheath School of Art, becoming by far the youngest student there. At Blackheath he soon discovered the joys of modelling and sculpture, his mentor being Frederick Halnon, formerly assistant to Alfred Druary, whose sculpture of Sir Joshua Reynolds stands in the courtyard of the Royal Academy. After a year at Blackheath, Skeaping moved on to Goldsmiths' College where he was the only day student in the sculpture school, all the young men having been called up for military service. From his early boyhood he had been fascinated by horses but he was now taking an interest in all animals and once a week he would visit the zoo to draw and model. He was particularly attracted to the big cats.

On leaving Goldsmiths' College he attended the Central School of Arts and Crafts. The life classes were particularly good there and among the models was a young Kenyan student of economics called Jomo Kenyatta. After two years at the Central School, Skeaping gained entry to the Royal Academy Schools where no fees were payable, an important consideration for his family, and where valuable prizes could be won. In his two years at the Royal Academy Schools he won every prize open to the sculpture students, culminating in the Royal Academy Gold Medal and Travelling Scholarship. His scholarship took him to Italy where he visited Rome, Naples, Siena and Florence. The last-named city held the greatest artistic fascination for him and he immersed himself in the culture of Michelangelo, Donatello and the other sculptors of their era. However the tragic death in Florence of a close friend and fellow student caused him to abandon his travels and return to England.

A short spell of teaching in Newcastle followed, but in 1924 he won the Prix de Rome and returned to that city on a three-year scholarship. The runner-up for the prize was Barbara Hepworth and, six months later, she also found herself in Italy on a travelling scholarship. The young English couple visited Siena together, fell in love and were married in Rome in 1925. They returned to England after nearly two years of married life, Skeaping needing treatment for the stomach trouble which was to plague him for the rest of his life.

Back in London, they took a studio in Chalk Farm. Skeaping worked mainly on carvings of birds and animals in Cornish serpentine while Barbara Hepworth's work, greatly influenced by Henry Moore, was more modern. However, after four years of marriage, the couple's artistic and temperamental differences – she was reclusive and ambitious, he gregarious and happy-go-lucky – drove them apart. After their divorce Barbara married Ben Nicholson.

During his marriage Skeaping had become involved with the Modern movement but now he reverted to a more realistic approach to his animal subjects. During the 'thirties he spent as much time as he could afford in the country, hunting in East Anglia, riding in races in Ireland and travelling in Provence and Spain with his second wife Morwenna Ward, whom he married in 1934. Morwenna's mother lent them

John Skeaping, *Hanging to the Left*, bronze.

a cottage on Dartmoor for their summer holidays and Skeaping spent months learning from local craftsmen the difficult and physically demanding challenge of granite carving. Granite is among the most arduous materials which a sculptor can choose because of its tremendous hardness: by the same token, the uncooperative nature of the stone means that there is a better chance of producing really good sculpture from it than from the softer stones.

Dartmoor and its inhabitants appealed to the gypsy in his soul and, when not working on his sculpture, Skeaping would ride for miles across the moor, pausing from time to time to fish for wild brown trout in the moorland streams. Dartmoor was also an excellent training ground for the greyhounds which he and Morwenna, a keen dog-breeder, started to race.

On the outbreak of World War II, Skeaping, who had learned to speak Italian fluently during his years in Italy, joined the Intelligence Corps. Sent out to North Africa with the First Army, he survived the sinking of the troopship *Strathallan* in the Mediterranean and took part in undercover work in Algiers. He then spent some time on

John Skeaping, *Upsides*, bronze.

counter-espionage in Spain before returning to England where he was engaged, amongst other things, in the interrogation of Italian prisoners of war. Later he transferred to the SAS whose individual approach to soldiering greatly suited his unconventional, fun-loving and irreverent temperament. However, his stomach trouble was aggravated by the nervous strain of his experiences and he was invalided out of the army shortly before the war ended.

His return to civilian life and London brought disillusionment when he failed to get back the teaching job at the Central School which he had held prior to the outbreak of hostilities. Like many returning servicemen, he found his place taken by one of 'the hard-faced men who have done well out of the war'. He therefore returned to Devon and bought a large house near Chagford, on the eastern edge of Dartmoor. The house was called Puggiestone, a corruption of the word Puckiestone or Fairy stone, because of a three hundred ton granite rock which lay beside the house, thrown there, so legend has it, by an enraged giant. Morwenna and their twin sons, who had been born in 1944, joined him at Puggiestone and Paul, his son by Barbara Hepworth, spent his summer holidays there.

Nevertheless the restless streak in his nature did not allow him to remain for long in his new home. Devon, though beautiful, seemed to him a cultural desert. He returned to London to teach sculpture at the Royal College of Art. In its turn London life now appeared to him artificial, pretentious and pseudo-intellectual and he therefore took leave of absence from his teaching and went to Mexico in 1949. He spent a year and a half there, living amongst the primitive Indians and re-examining his attitude to art and to life. He wrote of this period in *The Big Tree of Mexico*.

He then returned to the Royal College of Art where he became Professor of Sculpture, and his iconoclastic approach to teaching blew away many of the cobwebs then festooning that establishment. He proved an inspiring teacher and, with his Peter Pan quality of agelessness, always had a great rapport with the young. Although fond of quoting Degas's 'Art should never be encouraged', he did not live up to this motto. He became an Associate of the Royal Academy in 1951 and was elected to full member-ship in 1959, the year in which he was forced to give up teaching.

Although his base was still in Devon, he had been spending an increasing amount of time each year in Provence and in 1959 he bought a mill in Castries. This, once converted, was to become his home for the last two decades of his life. It lay close to the Camargue, that wild area of France which is a paradise for nature lovers and whose white horses were to prove a continuing inspiration for the artist. Here he lived in contentment with his third wife Maggie Scott, whom he married in 1969.

The first of the large bronzes which are the zenith of his achievement as a sculptor of Thoroughbreds was the life-sized figure of Hyperion commissioned by Lord Derby. This was a particular challenge because the little chestnut, winner of the 1933 Derby and St Leger, had died, at the age of thirty, six months before Skeaping was asked to start work. However the artist was able to obtain the great horse's skeleton from the Equine Research Station at Newmarket and he transported it to a house on Dart-moor where he was able to examine it in detail. After speaking to many who had known Hyperion and studying hundreds of photographs of the horse, he was able to complete the statue which can today be seen at Newmarket. The success of the Hyperion bronze led to further commissions and in 1965 Mr Stanhope Joel asked Skeaping to undertake another 'posthumous' bronze. The subject this time was the 1945 St Leger winner Chamossaire and the life-sized bronze of this son of Precipitation stands at the Snailwell Stud, Newmarket.

For his old friend John Hislop – the two had first met when serving in the SAS –

John Skeaping, *Secretariat*, bronze.

John Skeaping, *Mill Reef*, bronze.

John Skeaping, *Reaching for it.*

PLATE 9

John Skeaping, *Rounding the Turn.*

PLATE 10

Gilbert Holiday, *Epsom – Rounding Tattenham Corner.*

PLATE 11   Peter Biegel, *Slanting Down over Becher's . . . and the Next!!*

he completed a life-sized bronze of Brigadier Gerard. Skeaping at that time considered 'The Brigadier' to be the most beautiful horse he had seen but he was to amend this view when he saw his next subject, Key to the Mint. In his entertaining autobiography *Drawn From Life*, Skeaping writes of this horse, 'It was the first time in my long association with horses that I had seen a horse impossible to fault in any way'. Key to the Mint belonged to Mr Paul Mellon and among the other horses sculpted for this generous and philanthropic anglophile were Mill Reef and Fort Marcy. The bronze of the latter was the first sculpture Skeaping completed of a cantering horse. He derived particular pleasure from working for Paul Mellon and John Hislop because both men had an understanding not only of horses but also of art, a fairly rare combination.

During the last quarter century of his life Skeaping held regular exhibitions in London at Ackermann's. Outstanding among these was the retrospective exhibition of bronzes held at the gallery in 1979. Although best known for his bronzes, he was also a prolific draughtsman. His most successful drawings were in gouache or pastel and he succeeded brilliantly in capturing movement thanks to the freedom of his drawing and his economy of line (*see Plate 9*). A quick worker and one whose appetite for the good things of life frequently outpaced the funds available to acquire them, he often, however, gave way to the temptation to turn out drawings which fell short of the very high standard of which he was capable. His racing drawings were the most popular but his drawings of bullfighting scenes, Arab horses and trotting races were equally competent. His oil paintings, by comparison, seem stiff and less fluent than his drawings although good examples can be found.

In the best of his drawings Skeaping shows that he has few rivals when it comes to capturing the movement of his subjects. His line drawings can be superb and some outstanding examples are to be found in his illustrations for John Hislop's *Steeplechasing*, in my view the best book of instruction on the subject ever written. These drawings show his deep understanding of both horses and jockeyship.

John Skeaping died in the spring of 1980, six months after his retrospective bronze exhibition. Enthusiastic, gregarious and generous, he was a fine teacher and his influence, through his pupils and those whom he encouraged, will continue to be felt for many years to come.

Peter Biegel, *They Clotted my Crimson . . !*, detail.

SIX

Peter Biegel

During his long and exceptionally busy life Lionel Edwards took on only one pupil, Peter Biegel (1913–1987). Comparisons are frequently made between the work of the two artists and indeed the influence of Edwards can clearly be seen in Biegel's work. Edwards, however, preferred the hunting field to the racecourse and his pictures reflect this, whereas Biegel was equally at home on the gallops, the racecourse and when painting on different studs. Biegel's earlier work shows much of his master's influence but he soon developed a greater boldness and freedom than that of Edwards and these two qualities were particularly suited to the portrayal of the hurly burly of the racecourse.

Peter Biegel, one of five children of a Dutch father and an Anglo-Irish mother, was born at Croxley Green in Hertfordshire. He went to school at Downside where he broke the school 100 yards record and captained the 1st XV. From an early age he set his heart on becoming a sporting artist and, while still at Downside, wrote to Lionel Edwards. He enclosed a sketch with his letter and asked for criticism – and for a sketch in return. Edwards, who was well accustomed to such requests, replied and kindly sent the schoolboy a little sketch. We can imagine how greatly this was cherished.

On leaving Downside, Biegel bowed to parental pressure and reluctantly agreed to enter his father's iron and steel broking firm in the City. To the surprise of nobody, this work proved uncongenial. Apart from his latent ambition to be an artist, he had already become a keen foxhunter and, through the introduction of David Dale who trained jumpers at Seaford, had started to develop a love of racing which was to last throughout his life. His escape from the City came after the failure of his father's firm in 1935 and he joined Lucy Kemp-Welch's School of Art at Bushey. His studies there were interrupted by the outbreak of World War II during which he served with the 4th Battalion of the Wiltshire Regiment. Wounded in Normandy in 1944, he was later posted to Northern Ireland before being invalided out of the army in 1945.

On his return to civilian life Biegel resumed his artistic career and in 1947 he had a chance encounter which was to alter the course of his life. Summoned to attend a medical board, Biegel set out for London by train from Salisbury. Knowing that food would be difficult to obtain on the train, he had wisely equipped himself with sandwiches. One of his fellow travellers, a lean and fit sixty-nine-year-old, had not displayed such foresight and returned to their compartment in a mood of frustration after an abortive walk along the corridor in search of the non-existent restaurant car. Biegel generously offered to share his sandwiches with his companion, who turned out to be none other than his boyhood hero, Edwards. Edwards recommended that the younger man should first of all study figure drawing and that he would then be prepared to take him on as a pupil. Accordingly Biegel spent two terms at the Bournemouth School of Art, after which he joined Lionel Edwards at Buckholt, the latter's home in Hampshire, and there began his belated apprenticeship.

Edwards was one of the school which believes that genius, an attribute which he would never have dreamed of claiming, consisted of 'ten per cent inspiration and ninety per cent perspiration' and he proved a hard task master. He taught his pupil the importance of working quickly, from life and in the open air – regardless of the weather. This meant working at times in the bitter cold – and there were occasions when the studio at Buckholt was little warmer than the outside world because the Spartan Edwards, despite his age, seemed better able to resist the cold than many younger men. Aylmer Tryon recalls 'His studio was freezing. I insisted on a heater when the temperature was below zero. Lionel laughed at that and always referred to the heater as "the Aylmer".'

Biegel quickly learned the technique of capturing the English landscape with a minimum of fuss and he distilled into his pictures the feeling of mud and dampness which pervades the short days of our Northern winters. This feeling of authenticity which Edwards created in his hunting scenes soon found its way into Biegel's paintings of the Winter Game, by coincidence the title of his picture accepted by the Royal Academy in 1950. However Biegel was no slavish copyist of his master's methods and he soon established a style which was at once recognisable as his own. His palette tended to be brighter than that of Edwards and he worked with a freedom and boldness which Edwards never achieved.

In 1948, shortly after leaving Lionel Edwards, Biegel married Theodora Kennett, known to all as Dora. They had met initially in 1940, soon after he had volunteered for army service. Dora became an integral part of the team, accompanying her husband on many of his painting trips and taking care of his business interests.

The best of Peter Biegel's work was produced between 1950 and 1980. During this time he was greatly in demand to paint both hunting and racing commissions and for six years, starting in the late 'sixties, he spent two months of each year painting in the United States. He took the opportunity whenever possible of hunting in Pennsylvania during these visits. He also painted racing scenes in Italy, stallions in France

Peter Biegel, *Into the Last, Kelso*.

and made many painting excursions to Ireland. At home he held his first one-man show at Rowland Ward in Piccadilly and subsequent exhibitions were held at the Tryon Gallery. He contributed many designs to the Injured Jockeys' Fund for reproduction as Christmas cards and in 1987 the Fund reproduced seven of his pictures in its calendar.

Although he had carried out some commercial work and book illustration before the war, his best work in this field came from 1949 onwards when he was asked to illustrate a series of novels by Colin Davy, the Dick Francis of his generation. In 1950, Biegel published *Booted and Spurred: an Anthology of Riding*, which he selected, edited and illustrated. In 1965 he illustrated Ivor Herbert's *Point to Point*.

The work of many sporting artists this century has become familiar to the general public through the publication of prints of their work but in this respect Biegel has been badly served. One of the most attractive of the small number of Biegel prints in existence is of Winter Crop cantering, published by Rowland Ward in 1950. Winter Crop was trained by Walter Nightingall and won six races including the Rous Memorial Stakes.

The best opportunity which lovers of Biegel's work have of becoming familiar with his work is by studying *Peter Biegel's Racing Pictures*, published in 1983. This interesting

Peter Biegel, *Hurdle Racing at Leopardstown.*

book provides a representative cross-section of the artist's work but it has to be said that the very low standard of colour reproduction in the book does not do justice to his skill as a colourist.

For the best part of his painting life Biegel lived in Dorset, and many of his pictures of mares, foals and stallions were painted for patrons in the West Country. In these pictures he was particularly successful in capturing the rolling hills, small fields and deciduous woods of that part of England which he knew and loved so well.

The original home of the National Stud was in Dorset, near Gillingham. When it was decided in 1963 to concentrate the resources of the National Stud at Newmarket, the Gillingham stud was sold to Mr Simon Wingfield Digby who already owned much land in the area and was an enthusiastic thoroughbred breeder. Mr Wingfield Digby renamed his new purchase the Sandley Stud and became a prominent patron of Biegel; for him the artist painted the Sandley stallions Floribunda, Crozier and Porto Bello and also several attractive portraits of Sandley mares and foals.

Other West Country owners and breeders to commission Biegel included Mr Percival Williams, whose thirty-five year long mastership of the Four Burrow in Cornwall is the most famous in the history of that pack. When he gave up hunting he was given a mare by an aunt; this mare, named Aunt May, bred Mabel, winner of the Yorkshire Oaks, and the evergreen Be Hopeful, a stalwart campaigner for Peter Walwyn in his early days as a trainer. Biegel painted Aunt May and many of her descendants for the Williams family.

For Mr Bob McCreery he painted Camenae, the dam of the Two Thousand Guineas winner High Top, and for the Hon. James Morrison he painted the remarkable mare Set Free who became the dam of three classic winners, Juliette Marny, Julio Mariner and Scintillate. Biegel also painted the mares Lavant and Lucasland for their owner Mr John Baillie. Lavant holds the distinction of being admitted to the General Stud

62

Peter Biegel

Peter Biegel, *The Parade, Irish Sweeps Derby, 1971.*

Book because of the merit shown on the racecourse by her progeny, chief among whom were Lucasland and So Blessed, both winners of the July Cup. So Blessed also became a successful sire.

Mention has already been made of the artist's trips to the United States. Although many of the pictures he painted there were of hunting scenes, he also received commissions to paint several stallions; among these were Ribot, twice winner of the Prix de l'Arc de Triomphe, the Triple Crown winner Nijinsky and Secretariat, winner of the American Triple Crown.

When working on the racecourse, the artist has to sketch very quickly in order to capture the impression of what he has seen. These sketches may then form the bases for pictures to be painted later in the studio. A medium which Biegel used with great success, particularly when depicting racehorses and racing scenes, was a mixture of pencil and watercolour. Few artists have been better at evoking, with a few strokes of pencil or brush, the little actions which are at once recognised by those who have spent their lives among horses – the look of a mare towards her foal, a jockey knotting his reins in the paddock or altering his length at the start. These little sketches by Biegel are absolute gems and show better than anything how well he understood his subject.

One of his rare prints consists of little sketches of Lester Piggott's eight Derby winners. Another similar picture in pencil and watercolour shows the marvellous Epsom treble which Geoff Lewis achieved in 1971 when he won the Derby on Mill Reef, the Oaks on Altesse Royale and the Coronation Cup on Lupe. In 1973 Biegel was in action beside the paddock again at Ascot and he produced a sheet of charming studies of three of the winners at the Royal meeting that year, Abergwaun, Jacinth and Rheingold.

When asked to nominate his favourite racecourses, Biegel eschewed the more glamorous tracks such as Ascot, Goodwood or York and plumped for his local courses Salisbury (flat) and Wincanton (jumping). He painted many canvases of racing at Salisbury and the Cathedral spire, visible from the grandstand of this attractive course, can be seen in several of them.

In the early 'fifties the Biegels became very friendly with Peter Payne-Gallwey, who trained at Nine Yews, near Wimborne, only three miles from the Biegels' home. The artist's close involvement with steeplechasing dates from this period. He painted many pictures of the gallops and of Payne-Gallwey's horses; among these was the almost white Glenwood who won fourteen races and proved an excellent schoolmaster for the young Bob McCreery, a first-rate amateur rider before becoming the successful breeder he is today.

Among Lambourn trainers for whom the artist painted from this time on were Tim Forster, Fred Winter and Fulke Walwyn. In 1979 he painted a composite picture for Fred Winter's three daughters which they gave to their parents as a wedding anniversary present: this picture showed the heads of five of the greatest Winter winners, Bula, Crisp, Lanzarote, Midnight Court and Pendil. Fulke Walwyn has several Biegel pictures in his collection, among them a painting of the last fence at Cheltenham in the 1964 Gold Cup when Arkle beat Mill House. He also has a charming picture of those gallant veterans Mandarin and Taxidermist turned out in retirement at Saxon House.

The Grand National meeting at Liverpool acted as a magnet for Biegel and among the many good pictures he painted of the fearsome Aintree fences were a series of the unforgettable scene at the twenty-third fence in 1967, the year in which Foinavon finished alone (*see Plate 11*). The Biegels were well placed to witness this drama because they had taken their American friends Bob and Diana Crompton to watch the race from the Canal Turn stand. He also produced watercolours, now in the collection of Mr and Mrs Vincent O'Brien, of the remarkable hat-trick of Grand National winners sent over from County Tipperary by O'Brien. Early Mist (1953) is shown jumping the Canal Turn, Royal Tan (1954) is leading over Valentine's and Quare Times (1955) follows Sundew, the 1957 winner, over Becher's. On the subject of great steeplechasers, Biegel always maintained that, much as he loved Arkle, the greatest chaser he ever saw was Golden Miller. Following the historic day at Lingfield when the Queen Mother had a treble with Double Star, Laffy and The Rip, Biegel was asked to paint all three. He also painted the Royal corgis and won high praise from Lionel Edwards for his dog painting.

In an interview given in 1957 Biegel had some pertinent words to say on the difficulty of painting animals: 'Animal portraits are easy meat but an action painting may entail many days of arduous outdoor work often in the foulest winter weather; the

Leesa Sandys-Lumsdaine,
Mill Reef (Geoff Lewis).

PLATE 12

Raoul Millais,
An Autumn Day at Newmarket.

Michael Lyne, *Flat Racing Study*.

PLATE 13

Michael Lyne, *1965 Grand National: Canal Turn Second Time Round*.

scene has to be visited several times for background sketches to be made and days may be spent waiting for an effective sky and lighting conditions. The incident painted has to be fitted into the background and memorised in detail and sketches made on the spot to ensure the greatest possible accuracy – but it is fascinating work with many compensations. However, I think it would be difficult to get the feeling of the picture if you had never taken part yourself.'

It was in capturing this feeling of the racecourse that Peter Biegel's strength lay and he is, as a result, one of the most convincing painters of the racing scene which the twentieth century has produced.

Peter Biegel, *The First Fence, Mackeson Gold Cup, 1965, Cheltenham.*

Leesa Sandys-Lumsdaine, *Summer Silks*.

SEVEN

The Old Guard

T his chapter deals with a dozen artists born after the start of the century but before World War II. Some of them are still painting; others are sadly no longer with us.

Tom Carr (1912–1977) was born into a mining community in Co. Durham and worked initially as a colliery blacksmith. His constitution was not a robust one and in his mid-thirties he left the colliery and enrolled as an art student at King's College, Newcastle-upon-Tyne. His early days had not been easy and as a student he was forced by financial necessity to resort to unorthodox methods of obtaining painting materials.

In 1950 he started to earn his living as an artist, concentrating mainly on hunting scenes. However, he also produced many racing and point-to-point pictures, including some good action paintings of Aintree. He spent the last three years of his life living in the hills of Roxburghshire and until his death his reputation was mainly confined to north-east England and the Scottish borders. Since then, however, his pictures have gained a wider public and I feel that his work will be more keenly sought with the passing of time. His style is slightly reminiscent of Edwards and Biegel but is not of the same standard.

Another who spent her last years in the Border hills was Leesa Sandys-Lumsdaine (1936–1985). Born in Malvern, she spent much of her childhood in India, where her father was involved in the tea industry, and then returned to Worcestershire to attend Lawnside school. Brief periods in Switzerland and at Gloucestershire College of Art followed before she acquired a studio in Gloucestershire. A marvellous companion, her sense of fun pervaded her work and, like Snaffles, she became better known for her prints than for her originals. Few sporting artists have chosen better titles for pictures: *The Bride* shows an Irish farmer driving a cart which contains a sow, veiled under a pig net, on her way to a neighbouring boar; *The Roadhog* captures the chaos caused to some horses on road exercise when a young pig appears in their midst. Among her racing prints *Summer Silks* and *Winter Woollies* contrast the difference between

Leesa Sandys-Lumsdaine, *Absolute Heaven*.

flat racing and steeplechasing while *Absolute Heaven* and *Absolute Hell* emphasize how much more enjoyable a stable lad's work is in summer than in winter.

Sandys-Lumsdaine's work was shown in London at the Tryon Gallery – she and Susan Crawford shared an exhibition there at the start of their careers – and she received many commissions to paint well-known racehorses. Among these were the Derby winners Nijinsky and Mill Reef (*see Plate 12*), the Cheltenham Gold Cup winners Arkle, What A Myth and The Dikler and the Grand National winners E.S.B., Gay Trip and Nicolaus Silver.

The doyen of today's sporting artists is Raoul Millais who was born in 1901. He is the grandson of Sir John Everett Millais, one of the founders of the Pre-Raphaelite Brotherhood, and the son of the explorer, big game hunter, author and artist John Guille Millais. After leaving Winchester, Millais attended the Byam Shaw art school, studied anatomy under Frank Calderon, and attended the Royal Academy Schools where he was a contemporary of John Skeaping. In the early twenties he made a big game hunting trip to Africa and at one stage spent six months in Angola in search of the giant sable antelope.

After his marriage in 1926 he went to live in Gloucestershire and hunted with the Beaufort. He soon attracted the attention of several well-known figures in the hunting field and commissions followed. He took advantage of this, as Edwards had done before

Leesa Sandys-Lumsdaine, *Absolute Hell.*

him, to hunt with most of the packs in England until the outbreak of World War II when he joined the Scots Guards.

Millais also received racing commissions but he was fortunate in that his financial independence enabled him to be selective and he was not forced to turn out racing portrait after racing portrait. As a result, there is a refreshing breadth in the range of his work. He and his wife used to spend part of every year in Spain and some charming bullfighting sketches resulted from these stays. He also made frequent visits to the Scottish Highlands and his stalking pictures are much in demand. Many of his action racing pictures show the broad expanse of Newmarket Heath and his powerful skies are a feature of these paintings (*see Plate 12*). His early pictures often showed exaggeratedly tall figures and there is an elegance and style about his work which is a reflection of the artist himself. Among the classic winners which he painted were Big Game and Sun Chariot for King George VI and for Sir Winston Churchill he painted the gallant grey Colonist II.

Like his predecessor Edwards, Michael Lyne was never particularly attracted to the Turf, preferring hunting and the other traditional field sports. Born in 1912, he grew up in Herefordshire where his father was a country parson. On leaving school he determined to become an artist and his first recognition came in 1935 when he illustrated *Skilled Horsemanship* for Lt-Col S. G. Goldschmidt. The following year he founded and

69

Raoul Millais, *Premonition*.

Leesa Sandys-Lumsdaine, *Before the Start : King George VI and Queen Elizabeth Stakes, Ascot, 1969*.

Michael Lyne, *Cheltenham : Top of the Hill.*

Michael Lyne, *The Third Fence, Maryland Hunt Cup, 1966.*

hunted a pack of beagles but the pack had to be disbanded on the outbreak of war in 1939 when Lyne and his three brothers joined the army. During his time in the army Lyne at one stage found himself serving under Colonel Billy Whitbread whose firm later became one of the most generous sponsors of steeplechasing. He also worked for a time on camouflage projects with the landscape and marine painter Edward Seago. On demobilisation Lyne and his family lived in the Cotswolds and he held exhibitions in Bond Street. In 1950 he was invited to the United States to paint some of the fox-hound packs on the east coast and this visit was followed by several others. As a result he has, like Peter Biegel, a considerable following in North America.

The justification for his inclusion in this book lies in the series of paintings of steeplechases at Aintree which he produced between 1965 and 1975 (*see Plate 13*). Among the Liverpool heroes featured in these pictures are Highland Wedding, Rondetto, The Rip and Foinavon. He also, on his visits to the United States, painted several pictures of the Maryland Hunt Cup and one horse which he painted in both continents was Jay Trump, winner of both the Grand National and the Maryland Hunt Cup. Lyne's work varies enormously in quality but his best work can be very good indeed and it was sad that, having died on 20 March 1989, he did not live long enough to enjoy his retrospective exhibition which opened at the Tryon Gallery a fortnight later.

Lionel Hamilton-Renwick was born in 1919 and grew up in Northumberland where, as a child, he hunted. After the war he bought a farm in Sussex and started to breed Jerseys. His artistic début came about in an unusual way. On seeing some very moder-ate horse illustrations in a magazine called *Rally* he wrote to the editor to say 'My Jersey cows look more like horses than your illustrator's attempts'. As a result he was asked to draw a well-known horse each week for the magazine. This challenge inspired him to study seriously, first at Heatherly's, then at the Byam Shaw and later under the portrait painter Frederick Whiting. He sold his farm and held his first exhibition in 1953 at the Walker Galleries in Bond Street and subsequently held London exhibi-tions with Fores and Frost & Reed.

His racehorse commissions are invariably attractive and usually contain a feature of interest in addition to the main subject. One of his best paintings is a commission of Aureole, in the collection of Her Majesty the Queen. Among his other commissions have been Meadow Court, Roan Rocket, Grundy, Niniski and the fillies Fleet, Noblesse and Humble Duty. Hamilton-Renwick now lives near Newmarket where he breeds miniature Shetland ponies.

Another artist concentrating on equestrian portraits is Mara McGregor. She orig-inally painted only people but about twelve years ago also started to paint horses; the result is that she is now kept fully occupied with both types of portrait. Among

Lionel Hamilton-Renwick, *Start of a Hurdle Race, Plumpton*.

Mara McGregor, *Unite (Walter Swinburn)*.

John King, *The Irish Oaks, 1988*.

Barrie Linklater, *Special Cargo (Kevin Mooney)*.

Barrie Linklater, *Leaving the Paddock, Sandown*.

the best horses she has painted have been High Line, Habitat, Ardross, Dancing Brave and the Grand National winners Aldaniti and Last Suspect. Her most interesting commission was when she was invited to go to Canada by the Royal Ontario Jockey Club to paint Golden Choice, the winner of the 1986 Queen's Plate.

John King is an artist whose work is well-known to hunting men today. A keen foxhunter himself, he has received many hunting commissions both at home and in North America. He paints a smaller number of racing pictures, not unnaturally concentrating more on steeplechasing and point-to-pointing than flat racing. His work has been greatly influenced by Lionel Edwards.

Barrie Linklater is a thoroughly competent artist who did not start painting horses until he reached his forties. Having trained at the Woolwich Polytechnic School of Art, he emigrated to Australia in 1957 where he worked for four years as a freelance artist and illustrator. On his return to London he started to specialise in portraits of people and horses. He has painted several Royal commissions, including some interesting pictures done at the Royal mews, and his pictures of ceremonial military parades are convincing.

In recent years he has turned his attention to racing subjects (*see Plate 14*) and has spent time at various training stables, including that of Bill Wightman. His racing pictures, in my view, sometimes fail to capture the essence and quality of the thoroughbred in that his racehorses tend to look like hunters, albeit well-bred hunters. This is a criticism which could also be applied, though in lesser measure, to Leesa Sandys-Lumsdaine's racehorses.

An artist to whom this comment does not apply is Peter Howell who understands racing thoroughly, having worked in eight different racing stables, ridden over fences and held a National Hunt trainer's licence. Howell is an interesting artist and one whose work I enjoy a great deal. He has not been influenced one iota by the mainstream of British sporting art but has found his inspiration in the French Impressionists, notably Manet, Degas and Toulouse-Lautrec. Of the British painters, Bevan and the Camden Town Group have attracted him most.

From 1970 to 1975 he showed with Ackermann's in London but then found a more lucrative market in the United States where he has held frequent exhibitions, including an annual one at Saratoga. In 1988 he bought a farm in Kirkcudbrightshire from which he makes sorties to the training areas of England, France and North America.

His work clearly shows the influence of the Impressionists and his use of light and shade is full of interest. He succeeds in capturing the movement of racehorses and the atmosphere of the racecourse in a way which, in my experience, can seldom be achieved by someone who has not worked with and ridden racehorses (*see Plate 15*).

Peter Howell, *The Bottom of Warren Hill, Newmarket*.

Peter Howell, *Racing at Epsom*.

Neil Cawthorne, *At the Start, Cheltenham*.

To quote Munnings: 'He who paints people and horses must himself ride.'

Neil Cawthorne obeys this instruction, having hunted in his native Leicestershire and ridden out for many trainers. His early work was mainly of the hunting field but in recent years he has concentrated on racing scenes and now lives in Newmarket. His interest in racing subjects was given a fillip in 1971 when he was commissioned by the *Sporting Life* to paint Mill Reef and Brigadier Gerard and since then he has painted many classic winners. His work has been shown in England, Ireland, France and the United States.

Although this book inevitably considers the subject from a British viewpoint, I should perhaps give brief mention to a few foreign artists whose work is well-known in Britain.

Henry Koehler, *Study of Peter Greenall.*

79

Chief among these is the American Richard Stone Reeves who is one of the most popular equine portrait painters in the world. Indeed it has become almost a tradition for the owners of the top American horses to apply to have their horses painted by Stone Reeves. His portraits are excellent likenesses, containing the wealth of detail popular with the American public. To some European eyes this type of work is almost too photographic, but Stone Reeves's portraits will become a notable record of the great racehorses of his day in the same way that those of J. F. Herring, senior, did during the nineteenth century.

Henry Koehler exhibits frequently in London and his work is more in the traditional European style than that of any other contemporary American horse painter. The prices obtained by American artists at home makes it generally unattractive for them to attempt to sell their work in Europe where comparable pictures can be bought more cheaply. By the same token there are, I feel, some artists working in Britain today who would be better off financially if they were to heed the old advice to 'Go West, young man'. Of Koehler's paintings those which appeal most to me are his studies of jockeys and weighing room scenes.

The leading racing painter on the Continent is the German Klaus Philipp. A sound horseman who has ridden in races, Philipp understands his subject to the full. His work, however, is inconsistent and I know of few artists whose output varies so greatly in quality. His best pictures, the majority of which are in pastel, are, however, excellent.

Neil Cawthorne, *Three from Home, Cheltenham*.

Neil Cawthorne, *Arkle and Mill House, Cheltenham.*

PLATE 14

Barrie Linklater, *Fast Work on the Downs.*

Peter Howell, *The Water Jump, Liverpool.*

Peter Howell, *On the Turn, Ascot.*

PLATE 15

EIGHT

Susan Crawford and Peter Curling

Although it is too soon to pronounce a final judgement on the merit of those racing artists still alive – as George Washington's best biographer said, 'A tree is best measured when it is down' – I suggest that the two outstanding names among those born after the start of World War II are Susan Crawford and Peter Curling. The former is at her best when engaged on the formal, traditional racehorse portrait; the latter excels in capturing the movement of the thoroughbred in action.

Susan Crawford was born on 11 May 1941. Her father, Wilfrid Crawford, played rugby for Scotland, rode in point-to-points and served in the Royal Navy. When the war ended he bought a six hundred acre farm twenty miles east of Edinburgh, near Haddington. Here he and his wife Patricia brought up their family of three boys and one girl while, in addition to farming, he trained a small string of steeplechasers and hurdlers. As a trainer it was always his policy to encourage his stable lads in their ambition to become jockeys and among those who worked and rode for him was a strongly built lad from County Limerick, later to achieve fame as champion jockey, Ron Barry.

Susan Crawford thus grew up in a conventional country home where horses were an essential part of life, and her understanding of horses stems from this background. Art was also in her blood because her maternal great-uncle had shown considerable talent as a painter while Wilfrid Crawford's father was a talented watercolourist and an instructor in military drawing at Woolwich.

Although she received little artistic encouragement at school, she was determined to become an artist and, at the age of eighteen, rented a small flat in Edinburgh. For the next four years demand for her work increased and she received many commissions in Scotland, among them murals for a ship, a milk bar and the Forth Road Bridge Motel. Gradually her reputation spread south and she painted further murals in London for Selfridges and a night club.

At the age of twenty-two, deciding that she needed professional instruction, she

Susan Crawford, *Rummy's Final Becher's.*

Susan Crawford in her studio
with friends.

travelled to Florence where she studied under the renowned Signorina Simi for eighteen months. Her training consisted mainly of life drawing. The students would spend the mornings sketching nudes and the afternoons working on portraits, and they were encouraged to spend as much time as possible in the galleries of Florence studying the work of the Old Masters. The great portrait painter Annigoni befriended her but was absolutely mystified by her, to him, inexplicable desire to paint horses rather than humans.

The result of her sojourn in Florence was that she returned to Britain having learned to draw and with a great appreciation of the artistic traditions handed down over the centuries. Her studies of old men and women drawn in Florence gave her the grounding to become a successful portrait painter and her innate love of horses pointed her towards the field in which she was soon to become so skilled.

Susan Crawford left Italy in the late summer of 1965 and shortly afterwards went to Ireland where she painted Santa Claus, winner of the 1964 Derby and Irish Sweeps Derby. The picture was bought by Tim Rogers, at whose Airlie Stud the horse stood. Further commissions followed – Pall Mall, Soderini and the chaser Scottish Memories. While in Ireland she was able to ride every morning and paint during the afternoons and she still holds fond memories of this period of her life.

On leaving Ireland she moved to London and was lent by her friend and fellow artist Julian Barrow a Chelsea studio once used by John Singer Sargent. She was soon greatly in demand for further commissions; Santa Claus was followed by the 1968 Derby winner Sir Ivor and the champion hurdler Persian War. She also went to Vienna to do a series of paintings of the famous Lippizaners at the Spanish Riding School. Susan Crawford received great encouragement at this stage of her career from Aylmer Tryon and her first pictures were shown at his gallery in 1969. She moved to her own studio south of the Thames, near Albert Bridge, the following year and in 1972 held her first solo exhibition in London. The success of this exhibition naturally resulted in more commissions and a waiting list started to develop.

In 1974 Susan Crawford's life took a change of course when she married Jeremy Phipps, an officer serving in the Queen's Own Hussars. Since then their careers have flourished in tandem but her duties as the wife of a successful serving soldier have reduced the amount of time available to her for painting. Postings in Britain, Germany and the United States have widened the already large circle of Phipps friends and the arrival of children Jake and Jemma has made further demands on their mother's time and energy. The inevitable result of all this has led to the present situation in which the artist is forced with reluctance to turn away more commissions than she accepts.

Between 1970 and 1980 Susan Crawford painted ten Derby winners: Santa Claus, Sir Ivor, Blakeney, Mill Reef, Roberto, Nijinsky, Morston, Snow Night, Grundy and

Susan Crawford, *Two Unforgettable Show-Offs: Red Rum and Arkle.*

Susan Crawford, *Persian War.*

Susan Crawford, *Ela-Mana-Mou* (Willie Carson), detail.

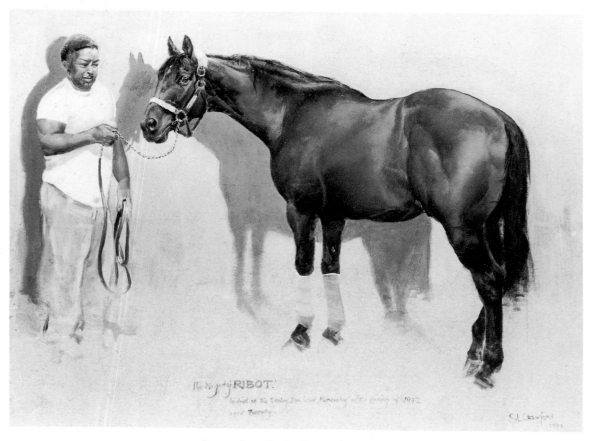

Susan Crawford, *The Mighty Ribot*.

Troy. In addition her skill as a portrait painter was recognised when she had the honour to paint many members of the Royal Family, including Her Majesty the Queen, the Prince of Wales, the Princess Royal, Princess Margaret and the Queen Mother. Lester Piggott has been a favourite subject and three of her pictures of the jockey have been reproduced as prints: *Assessing the Field* (Piggott on Park Top), *Masters at Work* (Vincent O'Brien talking to Piggott on Nijinsky) and *Lester on the Scales*. Among her other prints are *Arkle and Pat Taaffe*, *Red Rum on Southport Sands* and *The Mighty Ribot*.

Her popularity as a commission artist and the demands of her family mean that Susan Crawford's exhibitions are inevitably few and far between. Her most recent show was in 1980 and displayed the full range of her talents with oil paintings, drawings in watercolour, sanguine and pen and ink and a solitary bronze. The subjects included human portraits, equestrian portraits, military scenes, cattle, dogs and even African animals. One of the latter, a study of an inquisitive zebra, has the title '*Look! There's David Shepherd!*' During the last decade she has worked mainly on commissions adding,

Susan Crawford, *Arkle and Pat Taaffe*.

Susan Crawford, *Masters at Work: Vincent O'Brien,
Lester Piggott and Nijinsky*.

Susan Crawford, *Assessing the Field:
Lester Piggott on Park Top*, detail.

Susan Crawford, *Bustino: Special Treat.*

amongst others, Juliette Marny, Mrs Moss, Northern Dancer (*see Plate 16*), Slip Anchor and Dancing Brave to the list of famous horses she has painted. In North America she has painted Ribot, Arts and Letters, Relaxing, Stage Door Johnnie and Steady Growth.

Just as Terence Cuneo puts a mouse into many of his pictures, so Susan Crawford has a trademark in her most important works – a gremlin who is often engaged in some mischievous activity. Susan Crawford remains the leading living exponent of the British tradition of horse painting started by Stubbs and carried on by Marshall, Ferneley, Herring and Munnings.

Susan Crawford, *'The Race of the Century': Grundy (Pat Eddery) beats Bustino (Joe Mercer)
in the King George VI and Queen Elizabeth Diamond Stakes, 1975.*

PLATE 16

Susan Crawford, *Northern Dancer, the Daddy of 'em All.*

PLATE 17

Peter Curling, *Spring Drills*.

Peter Curling,
Maiden Hurdle, Clonmel.

PLATE 18

Peter Curling,
Has He Come too Soon?

The Irishman Peter Curling was born in Waterford in 1955 but was educated in England, first at Stonyhurst and subsequently at Millfield, to which school he won an art scholarship. It was at Millfield that he had his first experience of playing polo. In common with Susan Crawford, he also spent a period studying under Signorina Simi. Susan Crawford left Florence a disciple of the classical, traditional school of painting; Peter Curling, on the other hand, reacted quite differently. While grateful for all he learned there, particularly for the emphasis placed on drawing and on the development of the artist's sense of observation, he felt that students in Florence were trained too much to reproduce what was done centuries ago by the Old Masters. He decided that he must strive to say something newer in his work.

In this he was influenced by John Skeaping, with whom he spent a brief but important period in the Camargue towards the end of 1974. Skeaping impressed on him the need for an artist always to push himself to do something a little beyond what he has previously achieved. This is the most effective way of keeping at bay the ever-present danger of complacency. Curling sees himself not as a horse painter but as

Peter Curling in his studio.

Peter Curling, *Start of a Bumper*: number 8 carries the artist's colours.

Peter Curling, *Sprint Finish*.

Peter Curling riding his horse, Caddy, to victory at Limerick Junction, 1985.

a painter in whose work horses frequently appear. He has tremendous respect for Munnings, whose landscapes and bold use of colour he particularly admires, and for all those who, like his mentor Skeaping, take chances. He loves the work of the Impressionists – in particular Sisley, Degas and Monet – and tries, as they did, to capture the fleeting moment.

After his stay in the Camargue, Peter Curling returned to England and, while there, rode out on the Berkshire Downs and with Michael Stoute at Newmarket. He had his first exhibition in London at the very early age of twenty, when the Tryon Gallery gave him a one-man show. In the same year he returned to live in Ireland, first at Emo, near Port Laoise, later moving down to Co. Tipperary. His present home is ideally placed in the heart of the Golden Vale, for centuries the nursery of top-class thoroughbreds, and he is within easy reach of a handful of racecourses, including Limerick, Thurles, Clonmel and Tipperary.

Among the breeding establishments in the Golden Vale is the Orchardstown Stud, owned by the American Larry McCreery. It was here that Curling met his wife Adelia who had come over from the United States to work at the stud. She now provides the stable home background so essential for an artist whose work inevitably involves much travelling. They have three young children.

The largest and most demanding commission which Curling has so far undertaken has been for Vincent O'Brien's son-in-law, John Magnier, at Coolmore. It is a huge mural which covers one complete wall of a large cloakroom and which took the artist a year to complete. Finished in December 1984, it shows two hundred and eighty figures more or less well-known in racing on both sides of the Irish Sea. The artist's acute sense of observation has been given free rein and his skill as a caricaturist is here well exemplified. The drawing of cartoons plays an important part in Curling's life and he regards them not only as fun but as an important break between his bouts of more serious work.

Although he has painted a number of straightforward portraits of horses in training and stallions, many of them for John Magnier of Coolmore, Curling's most important contribution to racing art will, I feel, be his action pictures. One of his most successful action paintings to date has been of Prince Khalid Abdulla's Dancing Brave, ridden by Pat Eddery, winning the 1986 Prix de l'Arc de Triomphe at Longchamps.

His love of landscape painting and his keen observation, allied to his bold and free technique of painting, enable him to capture not only speed and movement but also the atmosphere of both the racecourse and the gallops. Indeed some of his happiest moments – and most successful pictures – are inspired by his early morning visits to the stables of Edward O'Grady who trains near Killenaule, ten miles from the artist's home.

Peter Curling, *Spencer's Bend*.

Peter Curling, *Ireland's Best*.

Peter Curling, *Tape Start, Clonmel.*

Curling is not afraid to work on a large scale and in his most recent exhibition, held in London in 1986, two of the best paintings were the two largest. *Spring Drills* shows four horses working on the all-weather gallop and was directly inspired by his morning visits to O'Grady (*see Plate 17*). *Sprint Finish*, a 48 × 72 in canvas, captures the drama and urgency of the subject, his blurring of the horses' limbs reflecting the technique pioneered sixty years earlier by Holiday. Another of Curling's strengths lies in his portrayal of jockeys and stable lads, and here he can draw on his own experience because he is one of the relatively small band of artists who have ridden a winner (*see page 91*). In 1985 he won a bumper race at Limerick Junction on his own horse Caddy, trained by O'Grady. His riding career was a short one because he found that the riding out, dieting and time required to achieve the fitness required for race riding took him away from his studio too much. Nowadays his adventures on horseback are confined to the hunting field in Tipperary and Limerick.

Peter Curling, *Thundering Hooves.*

Curling's early watercolours were more successful than his oils but he is now master of both media. Although he is still a young man, I shall be very surprised if he does not 'train on' to become one of the outstanding racing artists of the century.

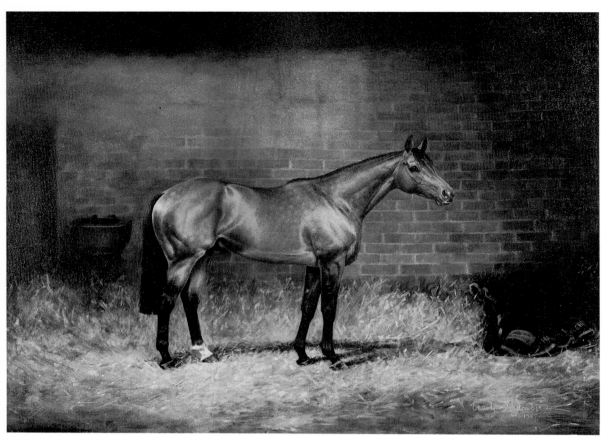

Carolyn Alexander, *Handy Proverb, Champion of Australia 1986*.

Carolyn Alexander, *Three Troikas (Freddie Head)*.

NINE

The Young Entry

A feature of the crop of racing painters born after 1940 is that most of the better ones are women. This is a break with tradition because in earlier days successful women artists were very much the exception rather than the rule.

Carolyn Alexander has the advantages of both breeding and environment for her chosen career. Her mother is the sculptor Peggy Alexander and she has lived all her life, except for a seven year period when the family moved to Glasgow, in or near Newmarket. Alexander rides out regularly with Henry Cecil's string and among other Newmarket trainers for whom she has ridden out are Tom Jones and Robert Armstrong. She is largely self-taught although she received help from John Skeaping, who advised her to rely as little as possible on the camera, and Richard Stone Reeves, who impressed upon her the need for self-discipline. Skeaping, the greatest teacher of his generation, also encouraged her to do action pictures and stressed how important it is for the artist to ride and to be as close as possible to horses in order to continue learning about them.

Because she has lived for many years at the centre of the British racing world, Alexander's work nowadays consists almost entirely of racehorse portraits. She travels a great deal and includes an annual May trip to the United States in her global itinerary. Her strength lies in capturing the likenesses of the horses she paints – landscapes and backgrounds do not come as easily to her as character studies of her subjects.

The list of owners and trainers for whom she has painted is an international one. For Raymond Guest she has painted a picture of Sir Ivor which the American gave to his trainer, Vincent O'Brien. For Alec Head she has painted Riverman and the Prix de l'Arc de Triomphe heroine Three Troikas. Another French patron for whom she has worked was Comte Roland de Chambure and among the horses painted for him were Arctic Tern, Bellypha, Fabulous Dancer and Luthier. Golden Fleece is one of many horses she has painted for Robert Sangster. Nor is her work confined to the northern

Claire-Eva Burton, *Turn for Home.*

hemisphere: she has in recent years made several trips to paint in Australia and South Africa.

An artist who concentrates on general racing scenes rather than on racehorse portraits is Claire-Eva Burton, whose home is in Kent. After studying at Medway College of Art – whose best-known former student is perhaps the dress designer Zandra Rhodes – she worked with a picture framer to supplement the income from the sale of her early racing pictures. She also rode out for the Epsom trainers Tommy Gosling and Mick Haynes. In 1986 Burton held a successful London exhibition at the Court Gallery and her most important commission has been to paint a series of twelve racing scenes for Her Majesty Queen Elizabeth the Queen Mother's box at Cheltenham. In her best oils she captures well the action and movement of the racecourse and her studies of jockeys, particularly at the finish of a race, are good.

Ruth Gibbons was born in Southport, studied at Southport School of Art and now lives in the Lancashire seaside town whose name has become synonymous with the Grand National legend Red Rum. After leaving art school she worked as an illustrator for the Royal Ordnance Factory but gave this up sixteen years ago and has since concentrated on equestrian pictures. She paints in the traditional style, of which Susan

Ruth Gibbons, *Fast Work on the Beach.*

Crawford is the leading contemporary exponent, and her portraits are attractive and competently painted. She has exhibited regularly in London but at present is in a position where the demand for her commissions is so great that she is having to turn work away. Among the notable racehorses Gibbons has painted are Grundy, Shirley Heights, Comanche Run (*see Plate 19*), Red Rum and the Champion hurdler Comedy of Errors.

During the past twenty years flat racing has become progressively less of a sport and more of a business. At the same time the leading owners have become far more internationally minded. Robert Sangster, from his base in the Isle of Man, started this trend and is still in the front rank of international owners and breeders. Stallions now travel from one hemisphere to the other to complete two covering seasons in one year, and racing in such countries as Australia, New Zealand, Hong Kong and South Africa thrives as never before. The prosperity of racing in any country seems, as a general rule, to be in inverse proportion to that country's tolerance of bookmakers.

Just as racing has become more international, so has the demand for racing art and today's artists have to be prepared to travel to an extent which previous generations would have found inconceivable. Crawford, Curling and Alexander are among the most travelled artists and the demand for their services is not only in the major racing countries of the world. Not long ago Curling flew to Zimbabwe to paint a series of racing pictures. This travelling, tiresome though it can become, is a necessary part of the development of an international reputation and certain artists who dislike leaving home, of whom Gibbons is an example, will remain less well known than their ability warrants.

The risks inherent in making too early an assessment of an artist's work are well illustrated by the case of Joy Hawken, who is still in her mid-thirties. Hawken was born in Northampton and had a thorough training as an artist with two years at Northampton School of Art, three at Leicester and a further year at the Royal Academy Schools where she won a scholarship for landscape painting. Her early work showed great promise, her watercolours, as is so often the case with young artists, being more assured than her oils. Like Biegel, many of her most attractive compositions are a combination of watercolour and pencil work.

Hawken has received commissions to paint several leading horses, among them Oh So Sharp and the St Leger winner Touching Wood. However, her more recent pictures have not always lived up to the promise she showed initially and her future career should be watched with interest. She remains a talented draughtswoman and there is time, if her work develops along the right lines, for her to reach high rank.

Susie Whitcombe, daughter of the Middlesex cricketer Philip Whitcombe, is three years younger than Hawken and also showed great early promise. Although self-taught, she grew up with animals and regularly rode racehorses while living in France. A seasoned traveller – she holds a private pilot's licence – she has held exhibitions in London, Melbourne and Tokyo. Her commissions include the flying Marwell, Pebbles and Jupiter Island and for the Queen Mother she has painted Insular, The Argonaut and Special Cargo. Whitcombe has now reached the difficult stage in many a woman artist's career when the demands of her young family leave her less time for painting

Joy Hawken, *Foals: December Sales.*

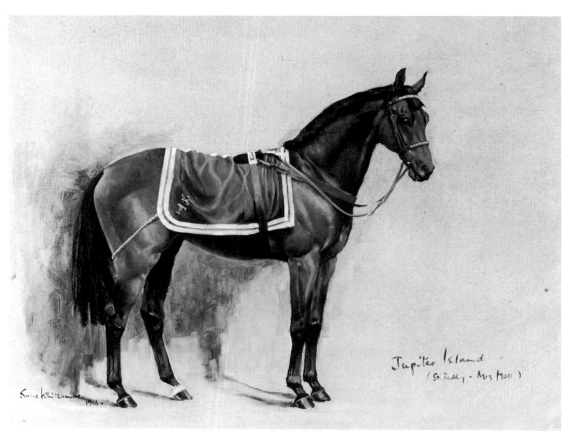

Susie Whitcombe, *Jupiter Island*.

Susie Whitcombe, *Pebbles and John Harkness*.

Adriana Zaefferer, *Northern Dancer*.

Mirjam Verhoeff, *Going Away from the Stands*.

than she would wish, but there is no reason why she should not in time establish herself as one of the leaders of her generation of racing painters.

Among the younger group of women artists are two who, although resident abroad, are well-known in this country. Mirjam Verhoeff studied at the Slade in London after initial training in her native Holland; she later continued her studies in Greece and Italy. Her love of horses blossomed after a visit in 1970 to work at the Spanish Riding School in Vienna. Her first major exhibition was at the Albertina Museum in that city and she has held subsequent exhibitions in Dublin and at the Oliver Swann Galleries in London. Verhoeff's work is at once recognisable. She works in crayon or mixed media on paper and her major pictures are seldom smaller than 30 × 36 in. She is fascinated by speed and conveys this with deft strokes of brush or pen, combined with a minimum of detail (*see Plate 21*). There is, on her own admission, an element of hit or miss about this technique but when it works the result is a powerful picture full of dynamic energy.

Adriana Zaefferer was born in Buenos Aires where her father is a surgeon. Her initial ambition was to be a vet but she decided to become an artist while still at school. She came to Europe at the age of nineteen, staying first in Switzerland with an aunt and later moving to Newmarket where she soon made friends with many leading figures in the racing world. For ten years she spent the summers in England, returning to Argentina each winter. During this time she was commissioned to paint many well-known horses, among them Alleged, Brigadier Gerard, Bustino, Forli, Grundy, Mill Reef, Pawneese, Northern Dancer, Shirley Heights and Thatch. Her earlier commissions were usually in crayon with little or no background but she now handles oils proficiently and has produced many good paintings of scenes on the racecourse and the gallops (*see Plate 20*). She has been greatly helped by the trainers Ian Balding and William Hastings-Bass, with whom she stays at Kingsclere and Newmarket respectively.

Zaefferer is another example of the new breed of peripatetic artist whose work is equally well known in London, Paris, New York or Buenos Aires. She and her husband have an *estancia* three hours north of Buenos Aires where she breeds polo ponies and stock horses but her commitment to her two young sons results in her being able to leave home less frequently than formerly.

While at present promising young women artists outnumber their male counterparts, the latter are well represented by Jay Kirkman and Tod Ramos. Kirkman was born in Los Angeles in 1958 and moved with his family to England when he was fifteen. Having studied at the West Surrey College of Art and at Camberwell, he started to concentrate on equestrian pictures in 1980. His best work to date has been in pastel and his large-scale pictures are outstanding. He is an artist who is temperamentally

Ruth Gibbons, *Commanche Run (Lester Piggott)*.

PLATE 19

Susie Whitcombe, *Riding Boy, Penang*.

Adriana Zaefferer, *On Warren Hill, Newmarket*.

PLATE 20

PLATE 21

Mirjam Verhoeff, *The Final Furlong*.

Jay Kirkman, *Hurdle Race, Newbury*.

PLATE 22

Philip Blacker, *Red Rum at Yeatman's Farm*, bronze.

Philip Blacker, *Racehorse from Another Angle*, bronze.

Jay Kirkman, *Early Morning, Lambourn.*

Jay Kirkman, *Going Down, Newmarket July Course.*

better suited by the freedom to paint whatever appeals to him than by the often limiting demands of commissioned work. Nevertheless he has produced successful portraits of the stallion Electric and the hurdler Ra Nova. He shared an exhibition with Adriana Zaefferer at the Tryon Gallery in 1988 and some of his larger pastels were very powerful, combining movement with the atmosphere of the racecourse and an impressive, at times threatening, sky (*see Plate 21*). The amount of work put into each picture ensures that he will never be too prolific, a fact which should make his pictures well worth collecting.

The final artist in this category, Tod Ramos, is the son of two artists, Theodore Ramos, the portrait painter, and Julia Rushbury. Born in London in 1956, Ramos studied art for seven years at Brighton, Gloucester and the Royal Academy Schools, leaving the latter in 1982. He has been involved with horses since his childhood and during his school holidays worked in Sussex for Gordon Smyth, who trained the 1966 Derby winner Charlottown before moving to Hong Kong where he trained with success until his retirement in 1988. Ramos rode out with 'Frenchie' Nicholson at Cheltenham

Jay Kirkman, *The Paddock, Windsor Evening Meeting.*

Tod Ramos, *The Arkle Bar, Cheltenham Festival.*

while studying at Gloucester College of Art and Design and many of his subsequent pictures have been painted under Cleeve Hill.

Ramos has held three exhibitions in London at the Richmond Gallery, the first one in 1985 being particularly successful. His oils are bold and his use of colour exciting, although some of his recent work appears to have been painted too hurriedly. A perceptive observer of the human characters who make up the racing circus, his most successful pictures are scenes of the paddock, the weighing room and the bars. From his home in Scotland he travels widely to attend meetings throughout Britain and Ireland. It is too early yet to pronounce judgment on the work of this convivial extrovert but there is no reason why he should not fulfil the promise demonstrated in his first exhibition.

Tod Ramos, *HM The Queen Arriving at Ascot.*

TEN

The Sculptors

Although (or perhaps because) interest in racing sculpture is now as great as it has been at any time since the heyday of *Les Animaliers* in the second half of the nineteenth century, it is surprising how much really bad sculpture is produced today. On this subject John Skeaping wrote the following memorable, and entirely justified, words some years ago:

> Since the last century, animal painting and sculpture has sadly degenerated, being now almost exclusively practised by unskilled amateurs who have no understanding of the meaning of art.
>
> The fact that such indifferent works find a ready market amongst a large section of the unknowledgeable public has encouraged more and more unskilled and untalented persons to try their hands at either painting or modelling, particularly of horses.

That such 'unskilled amateurs' should paint or draw is not surprising, given that the raw materials required for their work are relatively inexpensive. What I find astonishing is that so many people should go to the very considerable cost of having cast in bronze pieces which even someone with Nelson's eye for sculpture cannot fail to recognise as being totally devoid of anatomical or artistic merit. The reason for the high cost of contemporary bronzes lies in the fact that labour costs in bronze foundries have risen so greatly. Whereas during the last century labour was one of the smaller costs of the foundry process, today it has become the largest. With the casting costs of a single average-sized bronze of a horse now amounting to several hundred pounds, it can be seen how difficult it is for a young sculptor to become established.

Following the peaks reached by the French animal sculptors in the period 1830–1900, the art fell into decline. During the first half of this century Adrian Jones (1845–1938), the army vet best known for his fine quadriga *Peace* which stands at Hyde Park Corner, produced several good bronzes of racehorses. However, his work is less well-known than it deserves to be because most of his racehorse sculptures were

Adrian Jones, *Fred Archer on Ormonde*, bronze.

John Skeaping, *The Hurdler*, bronze.

Adrian Jones, *Persimmon as a Racehorse*, bronze.

John Skeaping, *Lester Piggott*, bronze.

commissioned portraits and were thus unique pieces or cast in very small editions.

Herbert Haseltine (1877–1962), the son of American parents, was born in Rome where he received his early education. He then went to Harvard, returning to Europe for further studies at the Royal Academy in Munich, under Professor Alessandro in Rome and at Julian's in Paris. He did not turn to sculpture until he was nearly thirty and one of his earliest commissions was of Spearmint, the winner of the 1906 Derby, for Major Eustace Loder. This fine portrait now stands in the Racing Museum at Saratoga.

In 1934 he was commissioned to produce quarter life sized bronzes of six famous American racehorses: Man O'War, Twenty Grand, Royal Minstrel, Billy Barton, Scally and Galahad III. Haseltine was thoroughly professional in his approach to sculpture, taking immense trouble to achieve a likeness of his subject. His professionalism is best illustrated by the story of how, when sculpting a bullfighting scene, he spent every afternoon for six weeks at the corrida in Madrid and then bought the carcase of the last bull he saw killed. As a model for the picador's emaciated mount he bought a broken down Paris cab horse which was in such poor condition that, after a fortnight, it could no longer stand and had to be destroyed.

Haseltine was a keen polo player and, in addition to his racing subjects, he produced many polo pieces and equestrian statues, among the latter being the memorials to George Washington in Washington Cathedral and to Field Marshal Sir John Dill in Arlington Cemetery. His bronzes are realistic and of fine quality and many of his smaller models were cast in silver.

The revival of interest in equestrian bronzes was led mainly by John Skeaping, an inspiring teacher and the most important sculptor of the century so far in this field. It would be hard to overestimate his influence on the two generations which have succeeded him (*see Chapter 5*).

There are a few sculptors at work today whose work is good, although at present lacking in that elusive quality of originality which turns the competent into the inspired. The senior figure among these is Amy Oxenbould, who was born in Heswall, Cheshire and whose very promising career – she won a scholarship in 1937 to study painting at Liverpool School of Art – was interrupted first by the war and then by the demands of family life. She did not start sculpting seriously until she was in her forties and her best work has been produced during the last ten years. Her horse portraits are accurate and lifelike and her most popular subjects have been polo and racing. Although her polo pieces are full of movement, her racehorses are usually more convincing in their slow paces than at full gallop. Among the horses which she has modelled have been the Derby winners Mill Reef and Troy and the champion hurdler Sea Pigeon.

Amy Oxenbould, *Foals at Play*, bronze.

Amy Oxenbould, *Sea Pigeon* (*J. J. O'Neill*), bronze.

Amy Oxenbould, *Paddock Study*, bronze.

Angela Conner's work is well-known both in Great Britain and in the United States where she won the international sculpture competition for an equine composition at Lexington, Kentucky airport. A friend of Elizabeth Frink, her work shows a comparable versatility and she is equally at home sculpting human portraits, equine studies or more abstract pieces whose impact is often increased by their interaction with light and water. She is one of the leading British breeders of Morgan horses, having a stud in Herefordshire, and among the best-known thoroughbreds which she has sculpted are Arkle, Persian War, Vaguely Noble, Blakeney and Park Top. She achieved an unusual double with the last named in that she also sculpted a fine head of the great mare's owner, the Duke of Devonshire.

Priscilla Hann is another competent sculptor whose own equestrian background lends authenticity to her work. A keen foxhunter, she was for a time secretary of the Albrighton. A graduate of Wolverhampton College of Art, she then spent a year at the Tyler School of Art in Philadelphia. To date she has concentrated more on

Angela Conner, *Young Lexington*, bronze.

Angela Conner, *Vaguely Noble*, bronze.

Gill Parker, *After the Gallops*, bronze.

Gill Parker, *Dancing Brave*, bronze.

Priscilla Hann, *The Winner's Enclosure*, bronze.

Priscilla Hann, *The Last Flight*, bronze.

steeplechasing than on flat racing; she has produced several convincing action pieces and an interesting study of the Grand National winner Aldaniti. Among the stallions she has sculpted are Solon Morn and Major Sol, both of whom stood under the Hunters' Improvement Society premium scheme.

Emma MacDermott had the advantage of growing up surrounded by horses in Ireland where her father hunted the Kildare hounds. She studied for three years in London at St Martin's School of Art and her range of subjects includes racehorses, polo ponies, dogs and children. Her work has been shown in Ireland, England, Germany and the United States and her most important commission to date has been a one-third life-sized bronze of Blue Wind for the Irish trainer Dermot Weld. Having youth on her side, it is to be anticipated that she will produce much more good sculpture before the century ends.

Gill Parker also belongs to the small band of young women sculptors currently producing good work. A self-taught artist, her work is shown at the Sladmore Gallery in London and in the recent past she has been commissioned to sculpt Precocious, Habibti, Rainbow Quest and Dancing Brave.

Another young, self-taught artist is Jonathan Knight who lives in Sussex where he and his wife keep and break horses. Many of his bronzes succeed in combining movement with accuracy and among his commissions have been Ardross, Chief Singer and Primo Dominie. His half life-sized bronze of Dawn Run, ridden by Jonjo O'Neill, stands in the enclosure at Cheltenham and racegoers can compare the difference in his technique with that of Doris Lindner (1896–1979), whose statue of Arkle is sited not far away.

Promising though some of these sculptors may be, I feel that none of them has as yet achieved anything to match the work done by Philip Blacker, the former steeplechase jockey who became a full-time sculptor on his retirement from race riding in 1982. During his career as a jockey he rode 329 winners and his last six seasons were spent as first jockey to the Lambourn trainer and former champion jockey Stan Mellor. I feel that Blacker is the one artist who is emerging as Skeaping's successor and who, in ten years' time, will be recognised as one of the major figures in twentieth century equestrian sculpture.

Although basically self-taught, Blacker has received help and guidance from Margot Dent, a former pupil of John Skeaping. His first one-man show at the Tryon Gallery in 1983 was an outstanding success and it was at once apparent that here was a major talent in the making. He succeeded in capturing the movement of his subjects, and his experience as a jockey gave him a feel for both horse and rider which is denied to those who have not ridden in races. Following his first exhibition, Blacker received many commissions to sculpt well-known horses. Some of these were static portraits

Jonathan Knight, *Lester Piggott : A Driving Finish*, bronze.

Jonathan Knight, *A Mistake at the Last*, bronze.

Philip Blacker, *Yearlings*, bronze.

Philip Blacker, *Going for the Line*, bronze.

in bronze while others were of horses in action, the branch of his art in which he most excels (*see Plate 22*). Among the horses he has sculpted are the steeplechaser Diamond Edge and such flat horses as Cormorant Wood, Pebbles and Lord Howard de Walden's Derby winner Slip Anchor.

In 1988 Blacker's most important sculpture to date was unveiled at Aintree. This is a life-sized bronze of Red Rum which was commissioned to commemorate the one hundred and fiftieth running of the Grand National. The sculptor took the view, correctly in my opinion, that to portray the horse with a jockey would diminish the horse's stature. Besides which, the question would have arisen as to which jockey to portray, both Brian Fletcher and Tommy Stack having won the Grand National on Red Rum. In the event the horse was sculpted with one foreleg raised and his courageous, intelligent head held high as he stares into the middle distance in an attitude which will at once be recognised by those who know Red Rum. A one-third life-sized model of this bronze (*see below*) formed the centrepiece of Blacker's second London exhibition.

What makes me suspect that Blacker will turn out to be, with Skeaping, one of the two most important racing sculptors of the second half of this century is the fact that he is constantly striving in his work to say something new. He has not fallen into the trap which claims many artists, that of churning out 'pot boilers' once a particular skill has been mastered. I shall be surprised and disappointed if he ever does.

Philip Blacker, *Red Rum*, bronze.

John King, *Becher's Brook, 1971 Grand National*.

122

Bibliography

Among books and articles consulted, the following were particularly interesting and helpful:

Aldin, Cecil, *Time I Was Dead*, Eyre & Spottiswoode Ltd, London, 1934.
Armour, George Denholm, *Bridle and Brush*, Eyre & Spottiswoode Ltd, London, 1937.
Biegel, Peter, *Peter Biegel's Racing Pictures*, Michael Joseph Ltd, London, 1983.
Blacker, Philip, *The Making of Red Rum*, Partridge Press Ltd, London, 1988.
Edwards, Lionel, *Scarlet and Corduroy*, Eyre & Spottiswoode Ltd, London, 1941.
    Reminiscences of a Sporting Artist, Putnam & Co, London, 1947.
Edwards, Marjorie, *Figures in a Landscape*, Regency Press (London & New York) Ltd, 1986.
Gordon, Adam Lindsay, *Sporting Verse*, Constable & Co Ltd, London, 1927.
Heron, Roy, *Cecil Aldin, the Story of a Sporting Artist*, Webb & Bower Ltd, 1981.
Marler, William, *Gilbert Holiday (1879–1937)*. Article published by the British Sporting Art Trust, 1983.
Masefield, John, *Right Royal*, William Heinemann Ltd, London, 1920.
Mitchell, Sally, *The Dictionary of British Equestrian Artists*, Antique Collectors Club, Woodbridge, Suffolk, 1985.
Munnings, Sir Alfred, *An Artist's Life*, Museum Press, 1950.
    The Second Burst, Museum Press, 1951.
    The Finish, Museum Press, 1952.
Ogilvie, Will H., *Galloping Shoes*, Constable & Co Ltd, London, 1922.
Skeaping, John, *Drawn From Life*, William Collins, 1977.
Walker, Stella A., *Sporting Art: England 1700–1900*, Studio Vista, London, 1972.
Watson, J.N.P., *Lionel Edwards, Master of the Sporting Scene*, Sportsman's Press, London, 1986.
Watson, J.N.P., (editor), *Collecting Sporting Art*, Sportsman's Press, London, 1988.

Mara McGregor, *Green Desert (Walter Swinburn)*.

Index